The Book of Jim

David Houck

The Book of Jim
ISBN: Softcover 978-1-955581-89-9

Parson's Porch Books is an imprint of Parson's Porch & Company (PP&C) in Cleveland, Tennessee. PP&C is an innovative organization which raises money by publishing books of noted authors, representing all genres. Its face and voice is **David Russell Tullock** (dtullock@parsonsporch.com).

Parson's Porch & Company *turns books into bread & milk* by sharing its profits with the poor.

www.parsonsporch.com

The Book of Jim

A Few Words About Jim

When my ol' buddy Jim told me he was going to write a book about some stuff that happened to us last fall, I have to tell you that it was hard to stop laughing. I mean, we all know that Preach (Jim, that is; he preaches some) can write a little, but a book? Who's going to read it? I said. You looked at any books lately? I said. They're all about sex and violence and money. You don't know nothing about any of them, and you wouldn't write about them if you did.

So now I've read the book, most of it anyway, and I'm not so sure. The boy has kind of surprised me. I mean, there's no violence in here at all, because there wasn't any, but there's some money and even a little sex - but just a little, mind you. Hey, like they say, it's all good.

So I don't know what to tell you. One thing is for sure. I didn't know he had it in him. Go see for yourself. Maybe there's hope for the boy yet.

Rain Upon the Earth

There are times when I walk surrounded by thunder. Where I go, the ground shakes. The air around me billows with acrid smoke. Two cars scream at the starting line. A sudden roar – unbearable, unbelievable – cuts through the smoke and the stink of burning rubber. Flames pierce the darkness.

The scream flees, fades, becomes a distant howl. The smoke remains, then slowly drifts away as two dots disappear down the racetrack. Behind barriers, the crowd shouts. Lights flash in the distance, red and glaring. Parachutes burst out from behind the receding dots. An announcer's voice begins to read off numbers.

I have been honored to start this first race of the day. Now I am alone in the middle of the track, with a starter's flag in my hand. The smoke is gone. The ground is still faintly throbbing, or that throbbing could be my heart. I walk back through the staging area, returning the flag to the regular starter as I pass, and go find Jack and Mike and our little hotrod back in the pit area.

This is what it should feel like at a drag race.

But not today. This late summer day was a washout. The rain didn't stop. Today's thunder came from the sky.

That night, Mike and I were outside our room at the quiet end of the motel, relaxing on those aluminum folding chairs. The activity near us was scant. There was our parking lot, a muddy ocean, without fish. There was the road, a dark glistening ribbon, without cars. Across the road was a gas station, without customers, then houses with no lights, and, about a block toward town, the neon sign of a diner, letters missing.

Say something? Sure, why not. "Looks possible for tomorrow," I said. Finish the thought. "Of course, that's what they said about today."

Mike shrugged. A blinking light high above the clouds traced a slow arc across the sky. When it disappeared over the horizon, I tried again.

"Thinking about Ol' JellyBelly?" Ol' JellyBelly was our nickname for our race car. Our hotrod. It had begun as a 1948 Fiat Topolino and was now a tiny red fiberglass coupe with gleaming chrome wheels and exhaust pipes and yellow flames that shot back along the sides. It had a Hilborn this and an Edelbrock that, and an engine that would take a whole page to describe, and I'd probably get most of it wrong anyway, but I was still fascinated by the yellow painted flames that billowed back from the engine and curled underneath the driver's window.

Mike slowly agreed. "Anyway, I'm glad we didn't race today."

"Really?"

"Car needs work." He shrugged. "We'll see tomorrow. Did what I could." He pushed his hair back. "Tightened everything. Lubed everything. Polished everything. We're about out of duct tape."

"I'll make a run into town tomorrow. Anything else we need?"

"I'll find out. Anyway, glad you're here," Mike said. "Hope you didn't come for nothing."

From the other side of town came a train whistle, and then, faintly, the rumble of railroad cars. They throbbed in the night for what seemed like a long time, and then there was quiet again. Past the diner that had the sign with the missing letters, the traffic light gleamed green, then yellow, then red, then back to green.

"You know what's funny? We drive a hundred miles, and we haven't gone anywhere. Look down the street and you'd think we're back in Taylor."

"No railroad," Mike said.

"So? Not exactly the same. Smells the same."

"You know what I'm thinking?" Mike said.

"What's that?"

"We need a better car. Got all winter."

"What's a better car?"

"Don't know. Maybe I'm just tired of this one. But this one's about done." He snorted. "It's coming apart. It's all just coming apart."

"What's that? The car? The season? The team? All of the above? Think Jack is up for funding a new one?"

He just chuckled. It was not a happy chuckle. Then he said, "Looks like the Barbara Jean Show has arrived."

A car was coming, a Ford Bronco. It bounced as it pulled off the highway and into our motel lot. I knew the car, and the driver, Barbara Jean Beltramba. A slender woman climbed out of the

Bronco and walked, limping slightly, across the muddy lot. She was wearing boots, jeans, a loose tee-shirt, and a baseball cap.

"Evening, guys," she said as she came up toward us. "We running tomorrow? Oh, hi, Preach, didn't see you at first. Going to have a prayer for us tomorrow?"

"Looks that way. Looks like we'll be running tomorrow."

"I'll be there for that. I like what you do. You have a way with words. Say, what about the cars? You guys watching cars tonight?" She wasn't asking if we were reviewing the passing traffic. She wanted to know if we or someone would be staying up to make sure no one messed with our vehicles, racing and otherwise, parked all around the lot.

"It's covered. We'll keep an eye on it. Go get your sleep."

"Thanks. What about that diner over there? Been down there yet?" She gestured down the street.

"Not this year."

"Don't blame you. Seen my rotten no-good husband anywhere?"

"Probably down there, at the noisy end. Everyone else that's awake is down there," I said, pointing to the far end of the motel, on the other side of the office.

"Gotcha. Do you know if he got us a room yet, or am I sleeping on the floor again?"

"Better go ask him."

Watching her heading down along the line of doors toward the far end, I said, "She can drive."

"You can say that again. Not too tough on the eyes, either. Her husband's a lucky guy."

"I hear she wants to start running on the circuit, and he doesn't want to leave the business," I said.

"She could make it. That'll be tough on him." He sat back. "Wonder if she'll need a mechanic."

"You're kidding. That's all you need."

"I'm kidding," Mike agreed.

A semi rig went by, slowing, brakes squeaking, as the stoplight past the diner turned red.

Then more light spilled out across the puddles when Barbara Jean opened the door at the far end.

The blare of a train whistle and then the faint throb of railroad cars came again out of the distance. They rumbled in the darkness, the sound ebbing and rising again, and then the sound was gone. One of the missing letters in the sign at the diner buzzed momentarily back to life, then went dark again. The traffic light flashed from red to green, then yellow, then back to red.

Light spilled out across the puddles when the door at the far end opened, Jack spilled out with it. He jogged around the puddles toward us.

"Come on over," Jack called. "You guys are missing all the fun."

"Fun?"

"You gotta be here." He was standing in front of us now. "Listen, come over. Little Mike, he's on a roll."

I looked over at Mike, then stood up. Mike didn't move. "Coming along?" I asked him. Since Jack was paying for all of this, I was thinking that the least we could do was humor him.

He shook his head. "Naw, you go. I might go over in a minute. I want to see them come roll up the sidewalks first."

A Great Light

Entering the room stunned me, for a moment -- the sudden glare, the onrushing billowing warmth, the smell of pizza, beer, sweat, and cigar smoke. I wanted to turn around and walk out, but Jack was already clearing a space on the couch for me in front of the television next to Little Mike, Mike's brother, who was glaring at a football game on the screen eight inches in front of him. The score was 21-3, Manila State up, with a first down on Bolivar's twenty-eight-yard line with three minutes left in the third quarter. This game was over, but it wasn't over for Little Mike. "C'mon, come oonnnn, you guys," he was muttering.

"What's going on?" I whispered to Jack.

"Don't know. He was watching the All-Nations Games when I went out to get you. He must have changed the channel," Jack whispered. Then, to Little Mike: "Mike, Mike. Jim is here."

Little Mike waved him off. He was transfixed by the game. "What are you guys thinking?" Little Mike said to the television set. "You gotta go to the run." He glanced over to me without seeing me. "These guys are gonna blow it, you just watch."

As my eyes adjusted to the light, I became aware of the other people in the room. Besides us, there was Barbara Jean, and Les from the Ace's Garage, and some people I didn't know who probably were from his current crew. They were lounging around a table by the refrigerator, drinking beer and talking. No one else was watching the television.

Les said, Hey, Preach, here you go, and handed me a glass of tomato juice. I would have preferred a beer, but Les didn't know me quite well enough to know that. I noticed that Barbara Jean's husband wasn't there. Uh, oh, I thought: Are those two going in different directions? There may be work for me with them down the line.

"We were just talking about the raceway sign, that folding one," said Les. "D'ja notice how it was all busted up? You know how they always have had it about five feet from the driveway? Well, the driver for that motorcycle team that came in about 1 o'clock? Musta not seen it in the dark and cut his turn too sharp, clipped it with his trailer."

"Are they the same guys who mashed up the sign at Crystal Spring a couple of years ago?" someone asked.

"Yeah, yeah, they sure were. They were running a Beeza then, one of them Gold Stars –"

"No, they weren't," said someone I didn't know. "They had that ---"

"No, it was the Beezer," Diane, Les's wife, said. "I remember. Because it was the time they had –"

"That's right, that's right," said Les. "But I thought it was that other bunch, the ones with the flag on their trailer. What was it, hon?"

A shout came from Little Mike. "What's this now?!" On the screen the referees were conferring. A penalty of some sort.

Les asked, "Heard anything new about the weather forecast for tomorrow?"

Jack said, "I'll find out. Hey, Mikey, can you find us the weather?"

Little Mike didn't answer. He was talking to the pom-pom girls splashing swirling masses of color all over the screen. "Look at her over there. No, that one. Yes, you. I'm talking about *you*! Look over here. Pul*eese*!"

Jack regarded him fondly, then said to the group. "Speaking of weather, you know that weather channel girl on the Capitol station? Well, d'ja know she was up here for two weeks last summer? I don't know where she was staying, but she came into our carwash, the one on McCollum Road. Would you believe she drives some beat up old Chevy? And she's really kind of rat-faced, not like she is on the TV."

"They say TV does that. Fills you out. Y'know, I met some big TV guy once, the news guy. Real rat-faced too, like you say. Nothing like how he really looks."

"She was staying in one of those apartments behind the garage on the old North Road," said Diane.

"That dump?"

"And she was with some guy. I heard she broke up with her husband. So maybe it was some boyfriend."

"The one she was with, or the one she broke up with?"

"Preach," Les said to me, "What do you think of this? What do you think this world is coming to?"

I got ready to say something, forming up my standard answer along the lines of tolerance and judge not, but Jack had reached over Little Mike's shoulder and turned the TV sound down. "Mikey, listen, what you were saying before, tell Preach here about your big idea."

Little Mike turned away from the commercial on the TV. He was puzzled. Big idea?

"You know, about the All-Nations Games and drag racing. Your big idea."

"Oh, yeah, those All-Nation Games." Little Mike switched the channel back to the Games. "Look at that," he said, without looking. "What are those sports they have? Who plays that junk? Water polo. Dance. Juggling. Shooting. Shooting while running. Shooting while skiing. Shooting while skiing and juggling. Shooting while riding a camel. Who cares about that garbage?" His fists were balled; he wanted to fight someone. "And look at those scores," he went on. "What kind of scores are those, you jerks! Go back to your jerkwater countries! What a bunch of phonies. How are things back in Lower Slobbovia? What's happening in Kickballistan? Just came over to stick it to Uncle Sam, huh? I mean, what *are* these scores. This is a ten!? That's a one!? A ten for the Slobs and a one for the Uncle, that's all they know, and that's the truth.'"

I was looking at the television. In the upper left of the screen was a tally of the victory medals won by the leading countries. The United States had as many medals as the next two countries combined.

"So what sports should we have?" said Jack, keeping Little Mike going. "What was your idea before?"

"Idea?"

"Yeah, like you said before. What did you say?"

Little Mike was puzzled.

"Something about making drag racing an official sport at the Games," Jack said helpfully. "Like, 'If we let them have their camel races, then why can't we have our hotrod drag races?' Something like that."

"Oh, sure! Right! Like any of those bums will go along with drag racing! Give me a break."

"Guys, Diane, Barbara Jean, listen to this," Jack addressed the group. "Little Mike thinks that drag racing should be an international sport. It should be in the All-Nations Games. Whaddya think?'

Everyone looked at Les, for some reason, maybe because he was the other team leader in the room. "Uhh, I don't know. Maybe."

"Hey," said Jack, "Drag racing would be good for these guys. They'd learn about cars, right?"

"Yeah …," Little Mike said tentatively.

"Sure, get 'em off their camels."

"Maybe you got a point there," said Les.

"That's right," Jack went on. "Get 'em into the modern age. Share with them. And think about this. We could sell 'em cars. They get rid of their camels; that's good for the environment. They open gas stations and repair shops; that's good for the economy. They make roads to whatever they got, rain forests or volcanoes or an oasis or old ruins; that's good for tourism. Hey, Mikey, I don't want to steal your idea. So, tell us, now what? Where do we go from here?"

"Whaddya asking me for?"

"You're not just going to quit there? Run your mouth and change the channel? Just quit?"

"Whaddya mean, quit? I'm not quitting. You calling me a quitter?" His fists were balled up again.

"Not quitting? All you're doing is sitting and yelling at a TV set."

"Yeah? What am I supposed to do?"

"Do something. Start a campaign or something."

"Who, me? Whaddya talking about?"

"So you just going to give up?"

"What am I supposed to do?"

"Nothing, I guess. Just go ahead and quit."

"If you're so smart, why don't you do it?"

"And steal your idea? Not me," Jack said, "Jim, help this guy out."

"Yeah, Preach, you can do stuff."

I didn't know what to say, but I wasn't about to get into the middle of this.

Little Mike went right on. "What would you do?"

"You know what you could do?" said Jack. "Have Jim here help you. Y'know, he could write something. Put it in when he writes up this weekend for the newspaper. Start writing some letters."

Write *who* a letter, I thought.

"What have you got to lose?" said Les, taking up the idea.

"We gotta do something," said the mechanic on the Ace's Garage team, playing along.

"Yeah, they don't let us girls play football, but we can drive cars," said Diane. "Look at Barbara Jean."

"Yeah, that's it," said Little Mike. "I'll write a letter. I'll put a bunch of letters out there. Preach will do it. You'll help me, right? I'll write a bunch of letters and send 'em to everybody. Call me a quitter!"

Jack stood up. "That's the idea. Little Mike is no quitter! C'mon everybody. Let's all stand up. Let's go on this. Let's take the pledge."

We all stood up. I was the last to stand.

"Go ahead," Jack said to Little Mike.

"Go ahead what?"

"Don't know. Are we quitters? Do we give up now?"

"WE DON'T QUIT!" shouted Little Mike.

"We don't quit!," we all echoed. We stood there proudly. Letters were going to be written to someone. We would all be strong for that. We glowed with the feeling that comes with accomplishment. We were already taking strong action. Beyond that, it seemed that we had done something else, although we weren't quite sure what. So we shouted it out once more, and then sat down to listen as the television finally cut away from the games to the weather forecast.

Still Waters

Sunday was beautiful, as promised, and we did run our races. I couldn't begin to start to write the letters I'd promised Jack and Little Mike, because I had no idea who to send them to, but I did do my 400 word writeup on the race results for the *Valley Trumpet* that night as soon as we got back to Taylor, even before I went to bed.

Monday I went back to work. Up here in the woods we have many hats, if we intend to survive. I write whenever I get the chance, and I have my -- what can I call it – Spiritual? Community service? Preaching? Anyway, I wear that hat on weekends, but during the week and for the next few weeks I would be wearing my carpenter hat every day, because it's carpentry that pays the bills around this house, and right now I had plenty of work. These days my main bill payer was a strip mall job about 40 miles north of Taylor, on the road between Stateline and Bigler. The job was steady work, through December, indoors, and most of the time I could work at my own pace.

That wasn't all I was doing, of course. In the shop I was working when time permitted on some fine cabinetry for a home office in a summer home over by Sadler, and in the house I was working on that second bathroom and thinking of looking around again for another house to rehab when spring came.

Then it was Thursday; time for my Thursday routine: On my way to the mall, I stopped off at the print shop to pick up this week's *Valley Trumpet* while it was still warm and with the ink barely dry, and talk shop with Morrie Morrison, the editor (and reporter, printer, proof reader, copy boy, janitor; also tutor at the high school and volunteer assistant one morning a week at the library). This Thursday there it was, the drag race report, right on page three top, but no graphic:

> The results are in from the drag race faceoffs held last weekend at the NaNo Motor Speedway in Redfield.
>
> There were no spirits – as in champagne-type spirits -- to dampen the brows of the Bedford County teams that competed, just a gusty rain that washed out all the

Saturday activities. On Sunday the local racers fared no better, as the victory champagne splashed over just about everyone except over the heads of the boys from Bedford.

Top laurels on the day went to Barbara Jean Beltramba from Pine Hill, whose Fantastic Plastic Forms dragster posted a blistering final 4.142-second, 284.75-mph pass. That speed was more than enough to hold off tire-smoking TV Tony Thompson and bring Beltramba the top prize of $750. Bedford County's own Don Wayne Johnston's best of 4.425 seconds at 269.43 mph was good enough to place him in the middle of the pack.

Also winning were Phil Porter of Union (Funny Car), Cap Fields of Pine Hill (Pro Stock), and Wayne Krejulic of China Flat (Pro Stock Motorcycle).

Other top showings from the local contingent came from Bobby Walker from Sadler, whose Ace's Garage '72 Camaro's times of 13.050 seconds and 97.862 mph were good enough for 2nd runner-up in the Stock Class, and Dale Mohacs' Jack's Car Wash '48 Fiat, from right here in Taylor, which posted a 9.597-second, 129.42 pass for 1st runner-up in the X/Hot Rod class.

"I knew we were up against it here at Redfield," an excited Bobby Walker said after the race. "They get some of the top talent in here from the entire Tri-State area, so you can't say enough about Les Stryker and the whole Ace's Garage crew and the job they did."

Local favorite Dale Mohacs narrowly missed edging Carl Beltramba's strong running '67 Plymouth. "The damp track conditions are really tough on a short-wheelbase car like ours, but our sponsor, Jack Van Dorn, and the Jack's Car Wash crew and especially our mechanic Mike Charney never stopped trying. We're all of us all fired up to come back next year and see what the new season will bring."

This is the end of the season for drag competition. Racing is scheduled to commence at the McCollum County Airport on McCollum Road next March 13.

"No graphic?" I asked Morrie.

Not this time. But yes, Morrie really did want 400 more words on this year's high school basketball team, and the more names, the better.

And, yes, the next time he was at the library he would see if he could find addresses of anyone that might be interested in promoting drag racing as an international sport, and what was that all about anyway? When I told him the story, he erupted in laughter. You said what? You promised to do what? The three of you and your little magic beat-up racecar? And then he started up again, so I told him I had to go, I was running late, and headed off to my job at the mall.

Saturday morning, sure enough, Morrie called with three addresses. By that afternoon, I had the letters done and gone. I thought that would be the end of it. I was wrong.

Where Your Treasure Is

About a week after we got back from Redfield, my friend at the lumberyard called to say they'd heard from a guy over by Bentonville who wanted some old logs removed from a drained pond. My friend said the sawmill was interested, but they didn't have anyone to go up and get the wood. Maybe I could go get it, and keep a log for myself?

I wasn't sure. Getting the wood wasn't going to be a problem, and I had the room to store logs, but I had enough already stored around the house, and what was I going to do with it? I had read somewhere that drowned wood was becoming popular, and music was somehow involved, but I didn't have enough time to go do the research.

Then my grown daughter, Erin, had an idea. When she called and I mentioned the wood, she said that a luthier friend of hers had been talking about acoustic possibilities of drowned wood. She would ask him about it and let me know the next time we talked.

So, the next week when the phone rang, I was expecting my daughter Erin with her weekly call. But it wasn't Erin this time, it was Jack.

He was excited. Jack is usually excited, but this was a whole new level, even for him.

"What are you doing home? You don't have work today? But that's good. Get over here. Come right now. Ya gotta see this."

I'm sure I said that I was in the middle of a project, because I always am, but he cut me off. "Don't tell anyone where you're going. Don't say hello to anyone. Got me? Anyone. Just get over here as quick as you can. I got something to show you. You won't believe it."

The carwash in Taylor is by the airport, just out of town on the McCollum Road. When I arrived, his car was in the lot.

Jack was waiting for me outside his office, at the door to a storeroom. "Get in here," he said, and shoved me into the storeroom. We sat inside there in total darkness for a few seconds. "Aw, poop!", he exploded, opened the door a crack, found the light switch on the outside wall.

He was holding a large manila envelope, and he was really excited.

"Oooeee, you're not going to believe this." He was bubbling. "Here," reaching into the envelope. "Read this."

"Nice paper," I said. I sat down on a box and started to read:

Institute for America
1 Reston Plaza
Fairwater, VA 22318

Taylor Racing Associates
James Lawrence, Secretary
63457 McCullum Road
Taylor, NA 50802

Dear Mr. Lawrence,

Thank you for your letter of 31 August. We wish to express our appreciation for contacting us.

As we understand it, you represent a group promoting the motor sport of drag racing, in which motor vehicles of various descriptions compete to determine how quickly they can accelerate over a measured course from a standing stop. In your words this sport exemplifies "the quintessential American virtues of individualism, ingenuity, mechanical aptitude, courage, and determination."

You are asking for our support of your proposal that the sport of drag racing be added to the athletic events in the All-Nations Games. In this way you believe that other nations and peoples will be brought to a greater appreciation of American core values, with the goal of emulating these values in their own cultures.

Mr. Ashhurst has instructed me to inform you, that this idea is of great interest to our organization. We intend to study it in depth and contact your organization in the near future with the goal of coordinating the promulgation of these great values that we all hold so deeply.

Again, let me express our appreciation for bringing this opportunity to our attention.

Yours very sincerely,
John A. Davidson
Institute for America

"Interesting."

"Yeah, yeah, interesting, huh? I'll show you interesting. Take a look at this." Jack pulled a press clipping out of the envelope.

"This is a picture of Miss Silver Spokes Wheel Cover, but it's torn off in the middle of her?"

"Not that, you goose. Turn it over."

I read: "'Drag racing is so quintessentially an American sport that I must question why we are failing to share it with the world,' Mr. N. Charles Ashhurst of the Institute for America announced to the Conference for American Values in Chicago on Friday. 'Are we ashamed? Don't we care? I propose that we begin planning to take steps immediately.' He announced that the Institute for America will be commencing a major effort to introduce drag racing to countries all over the world."

"Very interesting."

"Very interesting? Oh, baby, you ain't seen nothin'." Jack's face was radiant. His face could have lit the room. "You're not going to believe this." It was his 100-watt smirk.

He opened up the envelope, and then closed it. "I don't even believe it myself."

"There's something else in the envelope?"

"Oh come on. Can't you savor the moment? Show some interest, darn you. Sorry, shouldn't use those words. But listen, I don't even believe it myself, and you know me, I believe just about everything."

"Okay, I'm excited."

"More?"

"I'm really excited."

"Then get ready for this, baby." He pulled another piece of paper out of the envelope. It was a check.

"Now this *is* interesting," I said.

He sat back. "You! You know what your problem is? No sense of magic. No sense of theater. I see my work with you is not done." He leaned forward. "Because this is going to change everything. Feast your eyes on this."

He handed me the check.

It *was* a check, all right.

A check for one hundred thousand dollars.

I stared at the check. I thought I didn't care about money, but I have to admit that just this once I could not help but notice that bold, upright numeral 'one.' All those modest but self-assured little zeroes. "Lots of zeroes," I said, letting my breath out.

"What did I tell you? Go ahead and you hold it for a minute, then I want to hold it again."

I handed it back, speechless. I was stunned.

"So I need your help here. You're our treasurer. You think we can deposit this?"

"Uh .. "

"Look here." He pushed the check into my face. It was just a blur. "See? It's not right. First, they misspelled our address in the letter. It says McCullum Road. This is McCollum Road. And here. It's made out to the Taylor Racing Associates. Legally we're the Taylor Racing Association. But, it's signed. It's a real check. Look at this signature. Old Ashhurst himself put his pen to that paper. Good old Chuckie hisself."

This was all going too fast. I wanted to stand up and pace the floor, just to stop the tide, but the ceiling was so low I wondered if there might be something up there that would collide with my head. "Uh .. "

"See what you think of this. Here's my thinking. I've been thinking about it all morning. We need to get this thing deposited now. Whatever it takes. Right?"

"Well, --"

So here's my thinking. If you ever want to get something done and no questions, try sending the prettiest girl you can find to do it. I've seen it work. But we need to work fast, get this done now. Can you think of anyone? I know that finding pretty girls is a little out of your line, but we need to move on this. Maybe at the school? But they're in summer session, so that's out. Isn't it? What about your ministries? What about that beer ministry of yours? Or, somewhere? How about one of those window jobs you're always working on? Here's another one. Maybe Dale's sister? Daisy, I think. She's cute. Kind of skinny. Maybe too young?"

Dale Mohocs was our driver. His sister was a cheerleader over at the school and had done well in the chess tournament.

"She might be our best shot. So listen. How's this? We take her over to Luellen's. Facial, fancy haircut, nails, the whole deal. Luellen would do it quick, she owes me one. But suppose she wants a cut. People here are going to find out we got all this money, and you know these lazy kumquats will rob you if they can.

So, Luellen hits us up, charges us $30-40? Oh, brother." He shook his head. "Can you think of anyone else that's cute, willing, easily led? Or just pay the $40? Whaddya think? Or wait." He held his head and shook it, hard. "I think my brain just cracked."

"If y –"

"Cracked, but this just might work," he said. "How about we send Mike, and find a female teller?" (Did I mention that our mechanic Mike Charney is the rugged type -- husky, almost as tall as me, very good-looking?)

Jack was so far ahead of me. I just can't think that fast, and Jack at the moment couldn't think any slower. Finally I said, "If you're going to expect me to think too, can we get out of this storeroom? I can hardly stand up, and the chemical smell in here is making me woozy."

"Those chemicals are my fallback plan, Jim. When they're outlawed, this stash here is going to be worth a fortune. Here's my retirement fund, buddy."

But he got up, and we went down the hall to his office. Back in his office I started to breathe again. Through the hall window I could see a pickup truck coming down the line, covered with soap bubbles,. A man was watching the pickup truck the way you'd watch a newborn in the delivery room. I knew Little Mike was standing just beyond the end of the line, waiting outside with his rags to dry off the truck.

"Jack," I said, "It's lovely. It's nice. But, now, won't we have to do something?"

"Good ol' Jim, the deep thinker. Listen buddy, there's time for all that, but first, let's .. just … bank … that … check."

Jack went right on. "This is starting to give me ideas, you know. Maybe it's a sign to me! You know all about signs, right? Your big guy in the sky and all that. So maybe this is a sign to me, right? The golden path to wealth. I can almost see that path before me now, Jim. Cut this penny ante baloney. Think big! Take that ol' 24-carat flim-flam, dust 'er off, throw a little polish on 'er, wrap 'er up in Ol' Glory, and throw her out there for all the world to see! This deal is just a beginning, a drop in the bucket, Jimbo, just a starting point. A chance to practice. This check is just a drop in the pond, just the start of a mighty river. Outta my way. This crack brain is cracking' now. On our way to the stars. Before you know it, we'll be the biggest thing in Taylor. Then, Bedford County. Then, who knows? The whole Tri-State!"

I was thinking, It's no sign at all, except a sign that maybe you're finally losing it. This bunch – what's their name again? -- they must think we're some big deal. We're nobody, just three guys back in the bush with a beat-up old car and a typewriter. What happens when they find out we're Joe Blow from Kokomo? How are we ever going to deliver? But I couldn't get the words out fast enough.

"Whew," said Jack. "So you see the deal here. We need to get going, and pronto. So listen. Call Mike, or do you want me to call him myself? And, like you say, it's not too soon to start having some ideas. See what you can do about working up a budget."

Little Mike came back the other way. He waved as he went by.

"And we can start thinking about a business plan. One more thing. Once we've got these things going, we need to write these guys at the Institute, tell 'em about our progress and hit 'em up for more money. Face it, there's not much we can do with a measly one hundred grand. Now you got it? Let's talk in a couple of days. Want a soda?"

I was dismissed. Swept along by the tide. As always.

The Spirit Goes Where It May

Over the next few evenings I made time to try to come up with something for Jack. Of course I couldn't. I simply had no idea how to start. Jack said, just write something, anything. He said, see a travel agent, let them do the work. Go to the library, find a book. If nothing else, get a phone book and see if you can get the name of a consultant. What kind of consultant? Any kind, they're supposed to have ideas. And think about what you're going to write the Institute.

On Saturdays, I rest if I can, because Sundays I have work, even if it is the work of the Lord. (I don't preach, because we already have people around here who have regular congregations and I don't; what I do is bring the word and the sacrament to those who can't get to church: the firemen, the nurses and doctor at the clinic, the guy in the control tower at the airport, the field workers.) I should add that my Saturday 'rest' doesn't mean that I sit around, or nap, or meditate (although sometimes I do). It means I don't plan. I do whatever the Spirit moves me to do, and, this Saturday, the Spirit moved me to the county library.

But the library was a bust.

There was no listing for 'consultant' in any phone directory they had. Then I tried out an idea, the one idea I'd had so far. My idea was, put the money aside. Don't be thinking yet about how to spend it. If we want to spread drag racing around the world, we would sooner or later have to go to a place. What place would that be?

I wished Morrie was here to help me, but this was not his day. The librarians who were there did help. They started me off with an atlas, but between us we couldn't find anything in the whole library about drag racing. So I studied on that atlas until my head spun, there were so many countries. At the end of the day they agreed to let me take the atlas home so I could study on it some more.

Jack was pleased. Now we're getting somewhere, he said. He told me that he'd given the check to Mike in an envelope and told him it was probably better if he didn't look at it. When Mike came out of the bank, Jack asked him how it went, and Mike just smiled.

Meanwhile, there was the fellow over by Bentonville with the old wood. I took a day off from work and arranged for a flatbed truck with a ramp and a winch. When Little Mike and I drove over with the flatbed, he was telling me that Jack had been going crazy all that week, running all over the place, bouncing off the walls. He didn't know what had gotten into him, but even the customers were getting nervous, and could I come over and calm the guy down before he drove everyone around him nuts? I promised I would try but didn't say when.

At night I was making progress with the atlas.

I'd started with Asia and the East Pacific. Interesting, yes, but not cheap. I did a little investigation anyway. Of course the Asiatic mainland was impossible, if only because of the language barrier. There was Australia and also New Zealand, but the logistics of getting us and then Ol' JellyBelly there were probably going to be formidable. I made a mental note to keep the Aussies and Kiwis in mind.

Next was Europe. I'd always wanted to see France. I did know that there are a few problems with France. First, there's the French. Then there's the bureaucracy, which is also French. The food is weird, the prices are a little high, the language isn't English, everything's either old or broken or both, and I know I mentioned that they're French.

But I couldn't help but see that there were some offsets. First, the women are unbelievable, or so they say. Anyway, I can dream.

Second, they really know their racing. Over the years they've made some amazing cars. In fact, Russia may have invented the automobile, whatever, but eighty years ago, back at the turn of the century, France was making the most advanced cars in the world. They invented the overhead cam engine and a whole lot more. It was French cars that won every year at Indy when Indy first got started.

(I don't know what happened to them after that. Maybe they all got off into painting and rolling those funny cigarettes, but they still have some of the best racing in the world right now, even if none of it happens on tracks that are one quarter of a mile long.)

Third, if we want to go world-wide with drag racing, then France would be a place to start. Once France opens up, it's an easy step into every one of their old colonies and all the other Mediterranean countries. It would take time, and it wouldn't be easy, but I figured they might go for drag racing if someone were to show them they'd invented it. All we had to do now was to learn French, or find someone to go with us who could speak it.

So I filed that possibility and moved on.

For a couple of minutes I had the mad fantasy of Antarctica. All those penguins running around comically, and the seagulls. Even polar bears, if they have polar bears down there. I could just see it: cranking up Ol' JellyBelly, her screaming engine piercing the frigid crystal air, waves of massive avian flappery in every direction. Now *that* would be something to see.

But there wouldn't be any people in those frozen wastes to benefit from our abundant know-how, so getting more funding might be problematic, and environmentally it would be a disaster, and, of course, even getting there made getting to Australia look easy.

What about Africa? With unrest everywhere there? I didn't think so.

That left the Americas.

Canada I regretfully ruled out. Canada was certainly fertile ground for the long run, but it seemed to me we needed to start with something more exotic.

The time had come to get serious. We had to look south.

My choices were narrowing nicely. I decided I was looking for a place on the mainland, the closer the better. It would help if they would have some racing but no drags or just really primitive drags.

Mexico looked beautiful and exotic in the pictures. It was also close, and language wasn't going to be a problem; both me and Mike could speak a little Spanish.

It wasn't until my third review of the atlas that I noticed that there was a tiny nation in Central America where English was spoken: St. Guayábe. I had no idea it even existed. Looking back, and thinking about all that happened there, I find my ignorance hard to believe, but the fact is that until then I'd never heard of it.

That next morning I called the library. I needed to know more about drag racing today all over the Western Hemisphere, especially Mexico, and I needed to see if St. Guayábe was a possibility. They promised to call me as soon as they had searched their files and contacted the neighboring libraries to gather all the research material they could find.

A Tithe of a Tithe

Before the library called, I got another call from Jack. This was not the buoyant Jack of two weeks ago. This was the other Jack, the one whose dog had just died, whose newest car wash had gone up in flames, whose doctor had told him that he had to start to rest a little.

"Maybe you better get over here. Is this your beer ministry night? Can you skip it for once?"

"You got lucky, I was just headed out the door. What's up?"

"Maybe you better get over here."

"They wised up to us, eh?"

"Yeah, yeah," he said distractedly. "Can you just get here?"

He was in his office at the car wash when I arrived. The line was already closed and he was alone.

He leaned forward over his desk. "Here, check this." He read:

Institute for America
1 Reston Plaza
Fairwater, Virginia 22318

Taylor Racing Associates
James Lawrence, Secretary
63457 McCollum Road
Taylor, NA 50802

Dear Mr. Lawrence,

This is in reference to your letter of 31 August and our response of 19 September.

We deeply regret to inform you that a serious misunderstanding has occurred within our organiza ..

"Do I want to hear the rest of this?"

"Suit yourself."

He put the letter aside.

"I wonder if my ol' buddy Chuckie's still on the job," said Jack, chuckling grimly. "Poor ol' buddy Chuckster. Probably back up in his attic by now."

"Chuckie? Chuckster?"

"Mr. N. Charles Ashhurst? Our buddy at the Institute? Remember him? Maybe read the letter. You'll see."

He sat back and stared up at the ceiling. While he worked to build up suspense, I watched out the window. The lights down the road had already come on. I realized, too late, as I do every year, that the wonderful late light of summer had faded into fall.

Finally, I said, "I guess I should hear the rest of it."

"I do suppose. But suit yourself." He handed it to me.

Nice paper, I thought.

Dear Mr. Lawrence,

This is in reference to your letter of 31 August and our response of 19 September.

We deeply regret to inform you that a serious misunderstanding has occurred within our organization. It appears that a check may have inadvertently been included in our letter of 19 September. If this is the case, you are authorized by this letter to destroy the check. If the check by any chance may have been deposited, please contact me personally for further instructions. You may use the number on the business card enclosed.

Please be assured that this unfortunate occurrence in no way diminishes our interest in the project you have proposed. As soon as you have contacted our office, we will be more than happy to discuss with you the possible courses of our further cooperation.

We look forward to continuing this discussion with you at your very earliest opportunity.

Yours very sincerely,
John A. Davidson
Institute for America

He said, "I been thinking about this for two days. Day and night. I thought of everything."

"And?"

"You ever get to hold a check for a hunnert grand before?" He winced. "I mean, we had it. We had it right here in our hand. Right here. *In my hand.* I could see it. I could *smell* it. I could *taste* it."

I tried to comfort him. "Why is this such a big a deal for you? In the big scheme of things. I mean .. like, how much did you get when you sold your gas stations?

"That's different," said Jack. "That was my life's blood. This was a gift. It was manna from heaven. It was a sign, don't you see? Who knows? I might have actually started to believe. If you can believe that."

I wanted to tell Jack that I didn't see how this could be a sign, it doesn't work that way. Sure, money is all through Scriptures, but coming down? Was there any place, any place at all, in Scripture where God starts handing out money? Manna maybe, but has anyone ever seen manna on a menu?

"So I guess we have to return their money?"

"Yeah, I guess," Jack sighed. "Let me tell you the rest of the story. There's more."

When he had called them, Jack said, he made a point of asking the secretary if he could speak to Mr. N. Charles Ashhurst specifically. He was told that Mr. Ashhurst was unfortunately not available at the moment. Jack pressed. It appeared that Mr. Ashhurst was not in the office for the afternoon. It seemed that he was on a short vacation. In fact she wasn't quite sure when he would return.

Mr. Davidson on the other hand would certainly be happy to make himself available. In fact he was waiting for this call.

"That's when I got smart," Jack said. "I told her, 'Can you stay with me just a sec? Just one question. Won't take a minute. I'll be in your debt forever. Whatever, ever, I can do for you. My lips will be sealed forever. I'll send you roses. I'll donate to your favorite charity. If you can just answer me one simple short tiny little question.' And she said, 'Well ..'"

There were just the three of them. Mr. Davidson was his son-in-law. It turned out that Mr. Ashhurst had gotten a little dotty lately. They kept him out of the office and on the road as much as they could, but even that was starting to go sour. When he was around, they had a problem. They tried to keep the checkbook away from him, but he would just stay until they'd finally given up and gone home, and then he'd go through everything. In the morning she and Mr. Davidson would find long, detailed instructions on their desks. Thank God he didn't know how to get onto their new computerized system.

I was amazed that she told him all that. But I knew that Jack had a gift that way; people would talk to him. And I knew as treasurer of our little operation that I would be reimbursing Jack for roses.

When Mr. Davidson came on the line, Jack never let on, like he promised he wouldn't.

Mr. Davidson was brisk. He hoped they could work together. He was sorry about the misunderstanding. He hoped they could clear it up without any difficulties. Yes, at Jack's suggestion, he would be more than happy to send along a check for $10,000 to continue the project, as soon as they had their original check back. Some further discussion must have ensued, because, in fact, he'd be happy to have the check in the outgoing mail that day and trust our word as gentlemen that we would make the necessary arrangements concerning the original amount.

It was to be understood, however, that they were perfectly serious about this joint venture. They would expect a status report by return mail, and then every week until further notice. Mr. Davidson was quite firm about that.

"They trust us?" I was surprised.

"Jimbo, I know you'll never understand, but let me try to explain one more time. When you're already in for a hundred grand, what's another ten?"

"And now we send their hundred thousand back."

Jack exhaled. "Of course. We do have to do the right thing. Of course. And you'll get that status report back to them with it, right? Whatever else you do, let's keep these kumquats happy."

"I guess I see my part in things. A status report every week?"

"Whatever. Use your judgment. But listen, buddy boy, this is your time to shine. Sprinkle your magic dust on a few of these here status reports. There has to be writers out there who would kill for a gig like this. Set up a form, fill in the blanks, and let's see if we can rake in more loot."

"Until this Mr. Ashhurst dies, goes around the bend, or finds a new passion, I guess. You say he's out of the office for now? So we have no idea when or if he'll ever be back."

I don't think he heard me. He just continued, "So what do you think? Push 'em for money right away, or play it cool for starters? They might drop us if we push too hard at the get-go? Better to wait a bit, wouldn't you say? Until we can give 'em something positive?"

"I've been thinking …" I wanted to say that I may have found a place we could go. When we're sure about the place is when we start thinking about the money. Let the money grow from the plan, not the other way around. And there was another thought, just at the edge of my mind. Maybe this was a blessing, if any of this was a blessing. We weren't getting anywhere with $100,000 thinking, but $10,000 thinking was much more within our mental range.

But I couldn't get the words out fast enough.

"I've been doing some thinking too. So, say we play it straight. On the up and up. I don't see any other way, especially if you're going to be involved. That means we have to make it interesting for them. The more interesting we can make it, the more likely they'll stay at the table. So the plan has to really grab them. Once we have the hook into them, that's when we'll have to figure out what comes next."

"Yeah …."

"Oh, by the way, that check came in yesterday by express mail. I took care of it. Deposit slip's right here." He handed the slip to me. The deposit slip had today's date. "So, cut the big check back to them pronto. And, a status report, go with whatever we have. Now, ideas. Right now we have ten grand and no plan. Need the plan, buddy. This is big. Time is short. Do what you have to do. Find a place. Something really exotic, if you can. Let's get a trip out of this. Stick a pin in the map, if you have to, but find us something by Friday. I'll get Mike and Little Mike here at the carwash at 10 o'clock Friday, and we'll get this thing rolling."

Should I tell him I might already have a place? But, did I really? All I had was a name. What happens if I say something and Jack runs with it, which he probably will, and St. Guayábe is a bust? I needed to know more first.

"Can we make it a week from now? And a Saturday? If we're going away, I need time for research, and I still need all the workdays I can get." And I already knew I was probably going to lose one of those days doing research at the library.

"So, Saturday. But we're losing time here. Losing time, buddy."

"By the way, where is Little Mike? I haven't seen him lately."

"Aw, he took off a couple of days ago. Said he had a splitting headache. Something about too much stress around here. I don't know what he's talking about. I treat him like my own son."

Jack stood up. "You know, having less money is a good thing, in a way. Less money, less planning." He stopped at the door. "But we were so close to real money, Jim. This close. Well, like they say, one door closes, another door opens. Hey, can't sit here all day. Want me to grab a soda for you from the machine on my way back?"

"Sure. Make it diet."

Following Him

Dad used to have a saying: "When you go bear hunting, the first thing you need to know is, where's the bear?" As I entered the corner meeting room of the Library, was the bear here?

Half a dozen books and a large cardboard box piled up on a table were awaiting me.

As I stared at the stack on the table, I was hoping I sensed slowly gathering masses of dark and unknown shapes quietly swirling and merging, shifting, glowing intermittently, becoming ever darker and more threatening, growling ever more insistently in the recesses of my mind until at last they emerged into an enormous black pulsating cloud of hideous and glowering and flaming and horrible and chilling and altogether terrifying ursine mien.

In other words, if the bear wasn't here, I didn't have any idea where else to find one. If this St. Guayábe wasn't the answer, I wasn't going to have much to say at our Saturday meeting.

Right now, I knew almost nothing about St. Guayábe. This was not the only thing I knew almost nothing about. I didn't know how long we had for our safari. I didn't really know anything about the All-Nations Games, or the higher levels of the organizational structure of drag racing, or anything in any depth about any foreign country. I didn't know if we'd ever hear anything again from the Institute, I wondered about passports and travel restrictions. I knew my passport and Mike's were still good, because we'd gotten them the year before when we challenged each other to go on a mission trip and then didn't go, but I didn't know about Jack's or Little Mike's.

Time to get started. First, before I set forth into the ursine cloud, let's check my gear, find out if I'm ready. I opened my old leather briefcase and removed my library checklist, which I had carried ever since it was first printed in our high school newspaper:

- **Set out the notebook.**
- **Line up pens and pencil.**
- **Sharpen pencil if needed.**
- **Clean up the pencil shavings.**

• Deal myself a hand of solitaire. Keep playing until I win a game.

• Think.

• Take a break. Get a drink of water. Wander around in the stacks.

• Return to desk.

• Dither. Deal another hand of cards.

• Get to work! There is no time to waste!

Doesn't seem like there's time for cards today. Pausing only briefly to wonder how can a pencil that is never used ever need sharpening, I got started.

If you don't know why or where you're going, Mr. James, any road will take you there. I flipped a coin. Heads. Now what? Well, 'heads' has five letters. Quickly dividing the date of my birthday by five, taking the fifth digit from the result and multiplying it by the time on the clock, I rounded out the result and somehow arrived at the number six. I put my hand on the sixth book in the pile. It was a volume from an encyclopedia. Saying a quick prayer, I started reading.

ST. GUAYÁBE

ST. GUAYÁBE (pronounced *Goo-YAHB-ehy*) is a nation located on the northeastern coast of Central America. To the north St. Guayábe shares the Izturro Peninsula with Santa Albahaca. On the south and east it is bounded by the Caribbean Sea. To the west St. Guayábe is separated from Contraguas by the Alcama River and by the almost impenetrable Murracaino Swamp. Its mainland is about 190 km (120 mi) long and as much as 80 km (50 mi) wide at its widest point.

With 19,460 km^2 (7,550 mi^2) of land, not counting offshore islands, and a population of only 188,597, St. Guayábe has the lowest population density in Central America. Over 50% of the population is located in the capital region of New Hampton. Other important population centers are San Pecoris, known for its bone fishing and scuba diving, and Port Hueche, an industrial hub based on production of limestone and some powdered coral.

GEOGRAPHY. For its size, St. Guayábe is characterized by unusual geological diversity. In the **northwest** are volcanic crags, intrusive lava domes, and the Aguas Izturro International Reserve, a rainforest jointly administered by St. Guayábe, Santa Albahaca, and Contraguas. Ample rainfall creates a jungle-like setting — lush foliage, waterfalls and surging rivers. Because the Reserve is infested by poisonous snakes and inhabited by indigenous peoples who have had limited contact with the outside, it is yet to be extensively explored.

Along the **western** border and covering much of the far **south** is one of the world's largest mangrove swamps.

The **center** of St. Guayábe is dominated by the extensive Alakatries wasteland, a limestone plain also shown on some maps (ironically) as Sherman's Gardens. Running just offshore from San Pecoris to south of New Hampton, a distance of 100 km (65 mi), is the Guayávian Barrier Reef, a World Humanity Biocenter. The highest point in the country is located on the slope of Vincent's Crag, the peak (13,384 m, 8,465 ft) of which lies one-half mile northwest in neighboring Santa Albahaca.

CLIMATE. The climate of St. Guayábe is governed by its tropical location. During the hurricane season, St. Guayábe is lashed by storms, which periodically have caused significant damage. In 1978 Hurricane Josephine caused 11 deaths and over £80 m. in damage, particularly in the region around the capital, New Hampton. Temperatures throughout vary only slightly from day to night and from season to season, averaging about 25° Celsius (78° F).

GOVERNMENT AND POLITICS. The governmental structure of St. Guayábe today is strongly influenced by its complex colonial heritage. On paper an informal protectorate guided jointly by Britain and St. Albahaca, in practice it functions as an independent nation. The Governor General is appointed by the General Assembly from a list of three names supplied by the Royal House of Great Britain. Likewise, the Prime Minister is appointed from a list supplied by the government of St. Albahaca. Aside from these two appointments, neither country has any other official rights.

The Chamber of Notables and the General Assembly are the ruling bodies. In practice, the Chamber of Notables is a merely ceremonial body; power is exercised by the General Assembly. Membership in the General Assembly mirrors the makeup of the voting electorate, which is overwhelmingly English-speaking. However, all official business is conducted in both English and Spanish. Recently a movement has begun to include in some manner the third common language in the country, the local Creole known as Tok Kriolis.

HISTORY AND CULTURE. The earliest records, from European explorers who sailed along the coast in the 1550s, indicate indigenous settlement. By 1598 the Izturro expedition found only pirate infestations along the coast, which were eliminated. The expedition declared the area a Spanish colony but left no permanent habitations. For two hundred years, attempts to penetrate inland were largely defeated by disease, lack of water, venomous snakes, and high temperatures, but fishermen from several countries, escaped slaves, pirates, and mestizos collectively known as the Coastals established several ports, which have grown into the major cities of today. Around 1700 a limestone trade was established around Port Hueche in the south. A Spanish concession to allow the trade in exchange for British protection followed shortly. The expense of administration, poor prospects for further development, and the continuing hostility of the United States toward a European presence so near to New Orleans meant that neither nation took a leading interest in this challenging colony.

The outbreak of the Civil War to the north brought sudden and explosive change, as St. Guayábe quickly became a major center for smuggling supplies into the beleaguered Confederacy ...

I set the volume down. Now I knew something about the overall country. I wished I knew anything about prices, lodging, food, or local customs. I certainly knew nothing about any racing there. I didn't even know if they had cars, but I was going to find out.

A Box of Precious Ointment

Pushing the books aside, I opened the box and dove in.

After an hour and a half, I was still excited. Who cared that what I found was dated and often contradictory, almost Dickensonianly so. St.Guayábe was safe, it wasn't safe. It was healthy, it wasn't. It was primitive, it was comfortable and cosmopolitan. The economy was flourishing, the people were starving. But I didn't care, I had more knowledge!

I learned that the Governor General and the Prime Minister are by custom not on speaking terms. The Governor General will speak only English, and the Prime Minister will speak only Spanish. But then I found an encouraging clipping that commented that the two had lately been seen dining together at the Belvedere Golf Course, and that they had been able to agree on something, namely a choice of wine, of the type and vintage being promoted in an advertisement on the same page as the article.

I was concerned about the tarantulas, scorpions and snakes that were discussed in several places, especially the snakes. It seemed that there was an overabundance of snakes for such a small region, and especially an overabundance of poisonous snakes. There were eleven species in all, although the source was reassuring in pointing out that only seven were truly lethal, and, of those, only one whose bite was so lethal that the victim would probably be dead before hitting the ground. Unfortunately that one was the snake that was known to stalk its victims, even following them up trees to attack them. Fortunately most of those snakes were found almost entirely in the less settled central regions of the country or in the mountainous rain forest in the north.

The next folder on the stack was labelled **Old Confederate Days**, and it held some real possibilities.

I already knew that the outbreak of the Civil War to the north had brought sudden and explosive change to St. Guayábe. The country quickly became a major smuggling center. After the collapse of the Confederacy in 1865, fleeing Southern leaders attempted to rebuild their fortunes through the local economy. Cotton plantations had been established, but soon failed. A railroad built to link the shore settlements went bankrupt almost before it was completed.

Now here was an event to celebrate that heritage. I soon learned that Old Confederate Days is the Guayávian answer to Mardi Gras: a week-long riot of music, costumes, parades, foods from all over, a battle reenactment, celebrity guests, a fashion show, and more.

I was amazed by this event. Just the statistics of the festival were amazing. There are fewer than 200,000 people in all of St. Guayábe, but over a quarter million line the streets of New Hampton in the last week of February. Not a bed is empty and not a single anchorage is available in the entire country for the week of the event. Over 50 tons of costume jewelry is tossed into the crowd every year. Twenty-two million beer cans alone were cleaned up after the festivities ended. I skipped over the section on the total tonnage of the garbage, because I didn't want to know. And this: no fatalities, no serious injuries, only a handful of minor injuries, fewer than a hundred arrests and no one in jail for more than two nights.

Next in the folder was a schedule: Over the seven days there were four completely separate parades, with a day in between to allow for cleanup.

The first featured infantry reenactors, both Confederate and Union, led by the great Confederate cavalry leader J.E.B. Stuart on horseback, followed closely by a banjo player and a bones player also on horseback. Horses pulled artillery pieces and limber wagons past a reviewing stand under the watchful gaze of Confederate General Robert E. Lee, Confederate President Jefferson Davis, and even (since 1969) Abraham Lincoln. Marching bands boomed out military music. Aside from local units, contingents came from several U.S. states and even from Brazil. The parade concluded at a large field on the west side of town, where a mock battle was fought, artillery pieces were fired, and a competition of the bands was held.

And then there were the fabled '800.' As the story goes, when the major Confederate armies surrendered, approximately 2,000 Confederate soldiers refused to lay down their arms, preferring to march into Latin America "to find land, freedom, and glory." Thus began their epic battles against starvation, lethal snakes [again!], poisoned arrows, and fierce storms that left only 800 survivors.

This saga was captured in the popular 19th century novel *The 800,* which is now best remembered as the basis for the "classic 30's Hollywood film of the same name starring a stalwart Powell Henderson and the lovely and tempestuous Mary Maria Lupés."

I vaguely remembered having heard of the movie, but I doubt I ever saw it. The 'stalwart' Powell Henderson was just one of many indistinguishable images of stalwart movie heroes in my mind. But, from her many other movies, I certainly remembered the 'lovely and tempestuous' Mary Maria Lupés. She was often crouched, cat-like, and she was always intense, frowning. Her speech was quick and furious, faintly accented. Whenever she appeared on the scene, the men would stop whatever they were doing to pay attention to her. I always wondered what was wrong with her, and them. Why didn't she just relax once in a while? And now, I was going to actually see her, or someone who looked like her, and a Powell Henderson look-alike, leading some – all? -- of the 800 as their part of that first parade.

Two days later was the children's parade, and two days after that was the Mardi Gras celebration with music, dancing, and 'incredibly colorful' costumes.

The final parade was an informal affair that mocked everything that had gone before. Here were the motorized toilets and bathtubs, midget cars, cars that ran backwards for the entire parade, a walking performance of a full Shakespeare play, clowns, puppets, people dressed as prominent politicians who regaled the crowds with parodies of political speeches, dogs in costumes, electric rock bands powered by generators in wheelbarrows that followed them, and any other devilment that could be devised that could manage the two miles of the parade route.

Pictures of some of the vehicles in the parade showed cars that jumped, spun, twirled tassels, and careened crazily. One of these cars that had been featured in the parade five years before was especially spectacular. It was said to spin its doors and roof, explode, and then somehow transform itself back into a car. A note stuck to the picture advised that this car had been sufficiently dangerous in all its effects that it had not actually been paraded at all but simply displayed in the central square in New Hampton and then at the west field, where fascinated spectators could view its gyrations from a distance. I knew right away that I had to show all this to Mike.

Everything I saw – all the clippings, pamphlets, newspapers – agreed about the beaches. The traveler would be "blessed with expansive and unspoiled beaches, world-class scuba and free diving, sport fishing, and relative isolation." The Los Angeles Courier even described St. Guayábe as "the last undiscovered paradise for fearless travelers." Mind, I guessed, that this was merely wonderful promotional puffery, but such puffery takes on great force when one wants to believe it.

Here was a clipping about the beach bars. One was especially interesting to me, a cantina on one of the offshore islands near New Hampton named Rosey's World Peace & Love Shack.

According to this article, Rosey's was "the most laid-back island bar in the Caribbean, a classic ramshackle canvas awning, driftwood, and thatched roof menagerie on a classic palm-studded tropical island." Rosey's was known for its honor bar, its notorious 'Winter Games,' Rosey's hilarious impromptu ukulele ditties, the late-night ferry ride back to the mainland, and their slogan, 'Best sand in all the Caribbean.' Its signature drink, I learned, was the 'Pirates' Revenge,' featuring rum, lime, other fruit juices, cinnamon, and 'Rosey's special secret ingredients.'

By the time I had finished with the box, I knew that the official currency was the Guayávian pound sterling, which was pegged to the British pound; however, the American dollar was accepted in virtually all localities catering to tourists. I had several maps, notes on apartments and houses for rent, a short list of places to eat, and at least some information on local churches and transportation. I still had questions, of course. Where would we stay? What was the food like? How long were we staying, and what would we be doing when we got there? Most important, what was this place really like? I thought about the heat, and the safety, and the bureaucracy.

I never saw anything about any kind of race cars. What I did know was that the center of the country was mostly flat and nearly empty: even the scream of a 3,000 horsepower, 300-mph nitro-belching Top Fuel dragster would be swallowed up in the spacious (if occasionally lethal) tranquility of the central regions.

When I tried to tell Jack about what I had learned and what I hadn't, he didn't share my concerns. He wanted to know why it had taken so long for me to find a place. He reminded me about the Institute. He reconfirmed that we had a meeting coming up in two days. He said to stop worrying, because everything was going to be all right. We would just have to leave our cold winds and rainy weather and impending frigid snow behind us to endure being stuck with the swaying palms and the gentle tropic breezes, no matter how much of a hardship it might be for us.

Those nights, I was out on the porch swing, or on the grass, sitting under the stars in my aluminum chair, watching the sun set beyond the ridge.

I was thinking about what it might be like to leave the Valley. After all, I had work scheduled, and my ministries, and I'd been approached about making another run for the county Board of Supervisors. I'd never really left the Valley, except for short trips. What would leaving for an extended time be like?

All the same, I'd made a mental note to stop at the bank some morning to check the safe deposit box for my passport. But I didn't.

I was trying to think about 'signs' and 'calls.' Jack had talked about a 'sign.' Now, I know Jack was just saying that to get me involved, but I had to think, was all that money a sign, an attention-getter from above? What sort of sign could it be? His work somehow involves throwing $100,000, or even $10,000, at us so we can go running down to the tropics with fast cars? Somehow I doubted it, but who can say what His will is?

In the Bible, there's usually no mistaking a sign. A bush starts burning. The seas are parted. A blind man sees. A fleeing man gets swallowed by a great fish. But a check that arrives unexpectedly in the mail?

I also remembered that, in case the sign isn't enough, there'll be a call, the 'here I am' moment. The angel descends with a message. The clouds are split apart by a great voice. A plan unfolds in a dream.

So I waited under the stars. Tell me, is this Your will? You spoke to Jonah. You threw Paul off his horse. You sent a dream to Peter and an angel to Mary. Do you have a word or two for me?

Jonah. Jonah, from Scripture, how he was commanded by the Lord to go preach repentance to the sinful people of the great wicked city of Nineveh, and how he said, no way, I'm headed as far away from that place as I can get. So away he fled, but the Lord followed him to the sea, and sent a storm, and then sent the great fish to swallow him and vomit him out onto the shore, and he got the idea that, when the Lord tells you to go, you go.

Lord, you spoke to Jonah. Twice in fact. Even a murmur here would help. I said, do you want me to leave my work? My Sunday rounds? My beer ministry? My work with the kids at the school? My wife?

Even one word?

I'm leaving the valley and everything I know? To go where it's hot, and it's lush, and it's different?

And the snakes. Being chased by a snake? Lord, what about those snakes?

But the wind just blew where it may, and I got cold when the sun disappeared beyond the ridge, and, after a week of doubts and cloudless nights, I didn't know any more than I did when I started.

They Meet in One Accord

On that Saturday we convened at the office at the car wash at 9:58 AM. In attendance were our host Mr. Jackson Van Dorn, Mr. Michael Charney, and Mr. James Lawrence. (Mr. Michael Charney III -- Little Mike -- was outside as usual, actually doing the work.) After a brief social period with doughnuts, coffee, and tea, provided by our host and appreciated by all attendees, Mr. Lawrence was asked to open our meeting in prayer. Having done so, Mr. Lawrence was invited to make his presentation.

Mr. Lawrence commenced by saying that, if we were going anywhere at all, by far our best, and nearly our only, option was the small Caribbean nation of St. Guayábe.

Then, before I could talk about passports, point out how little I could really say at this point about practical living arrangements there, give my treasurer's report, or anything else, Mr. Van Dorn took the floor.

He expressed his appreciation and that of the whole group for all my hard work and quickly allayed the concerns I had mentioned regarding those practical living arrangements. He apologized for not having had the time to review all the materials in the folder I had given him, and he appreciated my diligence and my concerns.

He stated that the time had come to make decisions, to take the broad view, to push away the temptation to get lost in endless detail and research.

He pointed out, correctly, that the people there were able to survive. Therefore there had to be food, housing, transportation, basic sanitary facilities, and some form of entertainment. There would be work, certainly, but, being as our recommended locale was in the tropics, there probably would also be beaches, sun and sand, palms, and gentle tropical breezes. He speculated briefly on the possibility of encountering lovely, attractive, and willing native women, and quickly added that such individuals might well represent a missionary opportunity for me. We needed to resolve to leave our cold winds and rainy weather and impending frigid snow in spite of any sacrifice entailed.

Hearing no objection, he proposed that we move immediately to the main business of our meeting. He proceeded to outline the next immediate tasks. How long would we be there? Three weeks to a month; none of us could really be gone much longer than that. Did we have our shots? We needed to get them. What about passports? Not a problem, he knew a guy who owed him a favor that could take care of all of that. When would we leave? Aim for two-three weeks from now, before anyone had any second thoughts, and time enough for those passports and for any rescheduling of unavoidable personal or professional requirements.

Having established our timeline, Mr. Van Dorn then designated our individual responsibilities. Mr. Lawrence here was to hold the money and be in charge of the budget. The exact methods of accounting would be subject to his determination. As already mentioned, in addition to my continuing work at the library, I was to contact the Guayávian tourism office – there had to be one – in order to determine those remaining details of lodging, food, transportation, and amenities and attractions.

Once in St. Guayábe, Mr. Lawrence would be in charge of making the necessary contacts to further our mission – in particular, the connection with the Institute for America, submitting regular reports on our progress, being sure to address to them the need for additional funding. He will also monitor any domestic requirements as required on site to ensure our steady and secure maintenance, such as paying for lodging and restocking the food supply. "But you know what to do, I don't need to go into details here, do I?"

Turning to Mr. Charney, who had so far been entirely silent, he said that his responsibility will be to work with Mr. Lawrence regarding our actual mission accomplishment. Do they have any sort of motor sport? Any exotic cars? Any cars at all? What about possible places for a dragstrip, like airports? What kinds of garages? What other forms of entertainment were available, particularly competing forms of entertainment such as horse racing or field and track events? "Maybe they're into cock-fighting or something like that; who knows? We'll need to find that out, and that's where we're counting on you." He reiterated that Mr. Lawrence here will provide support as required.

Jack stopped here, but only for an instant. Yes, he said, and, before we go, we'll need to bring our young associate (meaning Little Mike) up to speed on the full operation of this facility. Do we even need to tell Mr. Charney, Jr., that we're going? Yes, we do, that's the right thing to do, and anyway sooner or later he'll realize that we are gone. But, he added, we don't need to go on and on about where we're going, though; he'll have enough to think about just keeping this place running without us.

As to himself, Mr. Van Dorn, having given the matter his long consideration, was offering to assume overall responsibility for the operation. He was willing to do the thinking, the coordination, the assignment of responsibilities, the high-level direction. He would take care of the passports. Once on location he would be the one to immerse himself in the local culture so as to anticipate any problems before they occurred and guide the operation through any treacherous cultural shoals or currents.

Concluding, he put forth the suggestion that we would meet again in two weeks to review progress and discuss the specifics that would be determined between this time point and the next. He then proposed to end the meeting, and, hearing no objection, asked Mr. Lawrence to close the meeting in prayer. Being somewhat stunned by the sheer energy and immediacy of his presentation, I did so, after which we were dismissed to go about our duties in preparation for our next meeting.

Through a Glass, Darkly

And I did; did go about my duties. That night, I had the snake dream.

I'm in a greenhouse, and I'm pretty sure it's the one that was behind grandpa's house. I'm calling it a greenhouse, because it's all windows for the walls and roof, but in the dream nothing about the greenhouse is green. It's all white, even the air inside – a hazy white, with fog or some kind of gauzy fabric, or both.

I'm walking slowly down the aisle of the greenhouse. There's a breeze – the fabric is swaying slightly – and I am aware of a faint hissing sound. It seems like there's someone ahead of me in the greenhouse, but I can't be sure.

I stop and look down. The floor around and behind me is seething with snakes. Snakes as large as tree branches and snakes no larger than worms. Some of the snakes are no more than dark shadows; others are lit up like neon, with glowing bands of black and red and orange. And all the snakes are white, even the neon ones; don't ask me how. They surround me on all sides, even hanging from the rafters. They seem totally unaware or uninterested in me.

Are they poisonous? Does it matter, if they ignore me? But suppose there is one up there, just one, that is waiting for me?

My feet aren't moving, but I'm moving. Directly in front of me, the path is clear. Everything in the greenhouse is flowing past me. It doesn't matter if I walk or not. I feel that someone is in front of me. Is there someone dressed from head to toe in white, or am I just seeing the fabric swaying in the breeze?

Carolyn? In her wedding dress? Or am I just dreaming? Well, uh, of course I'm dreaming; this is a dream. I'm chilled. I don't want to go on, and I do. Maybe I could turn around. Can I? I look back. The hissing sound has almost disappeared. Everything behind me has disappeared into the fog. The snakes are gone. I start moving again, very slowly. At one point I lose patience and try to run, but I can't, there's something that tugs at me, blocking me, holding me back. No matter; I never get any closer, never find out for sure whether there's someone ahead of me or not.

I had been thinking about finding a house or a cabin to work on during the winter. There were enough of them around. I did look at one, but decided it was too far away.

Erin came, liked the wood I'd bought, the submerged wood, and wanted me to cut billets for her. She was in a hurry; no time to come to the cemetery with me.

Jack found a house in St. Guayábe that we could rent for a month from the list of phone numbers he'd taken from me.

Little Mike found a guy waiting in the carwash line who'd *actually been* to St. Guayábe. The guy said it was a paradise.

Mike had been spreading the word around his mechanic friends. He thought he had a lead on a job down there.

And I couldn't quite get rid of that hissing sound.

At the diner my sausage omelet was superb, as always.

Mabel was curling up on my lap when I read the newspaper on the couch.

The wind skidded a can across the road outside the porch.

I didn't go to the bank for my passport again.

I picked up an old rose and left a new one. Move on.

Then the cats got loud, Mabel and Mildred.

In town, the storefront chapel was quiet, but their sign got loud.

At the market, the milk was loud.

I sat on my lawn chair in the back yard. The sun broke over the Polfuss place in the morning. In the evening the fireflies were gone. The garden was loud. The sky was loud.

I wished I could go to the Buckhorn. The Buckhorn was a bar/restaurant about 25 miles east of Taylor, at StateLine. Almost every Friday night a wise pastor was there to talk, listen, or simply offer quiet company.

Unfortunately, that wise pastor would be me, and that was my beer ministry. So that option was out.

I did think this. Suppose that wise pastor at the Buckhorn wasn't me. What advice would he give me? Knowing him, and I did, he probably wouldn't say anything. He'd listen. Clarify if necessary. Ask for specifics. Hopefully let me find out for myself that I might already have an answer, even if it wasn't the answer I wanted.

And I knew this: I did have an answer, even if I didn't want to know I had an answer.

Fine advice there; now can I apply it to myself? Can I allow myself to be that selfish?

Spreading the Ointment

Mike and I were finally able to get together at the diner to go over the responsibilities that Jack had assigned him in the meeting. When I gave him the folders of what I had found, Mike couldn't stop going through the pictures of the cars.

"Look at this! How do you make a car do that?" He was staring at the picture spread of the car with the revolving doors and exploding roof. "That's amazing."

He took the pad of paper I had brought and started making sketches and notes. (I saved one of them. Toward the upper left corner was written 'engine,' with an arrow down to a scrawl. 'Tube frame,' over there, with another arrow. 'What thicknesses?' and 'Doors? Lime green? Artwork? Local artist?')

As he went, he explained to me in bursts of words what he was thinking; most of it went right by me.

"How much would this cost?"

"Who cares? We can't do it. Not on the money we have. But, maybe we can. It won't be cheap." He started drawing on the pad. "Hydraulic pumps, they cost. It'll need good ones. The whole system." More arrows and shapes rapidly appeared on his pad. "How do you control all this? Remote? How do you do that?" He looked up. "Wow, I don't know much. We'll have to get some catalogs. How about a sound system? I'll give you a list of what we need, and you can cost it out. You think the Institute will buy that? Can you try them?"

With a last look, he pushed the drawings aside. "I don't want to take our car down there," he said. "Not just yet. Maybe just start something? I start a build, and you show it around. Maybe we can find some other backers?"

We went through the folders. We soon saw that they certainly did have cars. They had Old Confederate Days – all kinds of cars there. They also had fishing and scuba diving, and research opportunities to study their spectacular reefs, but we didn't find anything on drag racing, or any motor sports, or cockfighting.

Long after I was ready to move on, Mike was carefully studying every piece of information in the folders, reading every brochure and both sides of every clipping.

I wanted to tell him what I was thinking that I wasn't sure I was going to make the trip, but he was so focused on planning that I just couldn't do it.

That night, as I lay abed, my questions loomed large. They loomed in the gloom. Was there room for a loom in the gloom? Need a broom? Here's a broom to sweep away the gloom that looms in the room.

I'm not going.

That next morning I was sitting at the dining room table with my journal. The hissing sound was gone.

How to tell them?

My first thought was just not to show up when they left, but that seemed too abrupt.

I've got it. I'll show up but tell them I have a headache. Or, a job just came up. One of the cats is sick or might get sick. I forgot some work I need to do in the garden. They can't spare me at the mall. I need to be here Tuesday to take a rose to Carolyn at the cemetery. There, that's what I can tell them. Sure I can.

When I'd amused myself sufficiently, I got serious.

Lord, if you want me to go, I'll go. But I really want that sign. Something umistakeable. Like a voice in the cloud. A great storm. Maybe a response from the Institute?

I went to dad. He said, okay, Mr. James, time to cut the nonsense and get off the pot.

Carolyn was no help. She said, it's all right, I can live without a rose for a month.

(She can live? Live? What's that about? There may be some work I need to do here.)

The wise pastor took in all the words and the thoughts. He said, you know what you have to do. When you're ready, just do it, and move on.

So I did it. I called Mike, and told him. Then I called Jack. He'd come across Rosey's World Peace & Love Shack in the folder, and was raving about the sand, and the honor bar, and the times we were going to have. I knew he didn't hear what I had said.

The Eleventh Hour

Saturday morning Jack had again set out pastries, coffee, and (for me) tea. This meeting was not as formal as the last one; Jack was still too excited. He couldn't stop talking about Rosey's. "Do you see what he's got here?" He was holding out the copy of an article that had been in the folder I'd given him. "He says here he's got the best sand in all St. Guayábe. I'm going to start advertising that I have the best water in Bedford County. I can learn from this man!"

Little Mike was excited too. He was getting an extra $2 an hour to be the acting manager.

Mike quietly showed us his revised car plans and talked about a possible workspace he'd heard of in an area in or near New Hampton called Canaltown. (I had to confess I'd never come across 'Canaltown' in my research.)

We went over the money, and the house, and the budget I'd prepared. I noted that I was not able to locate a Guayávian tourist office. It was moved and accepted that Mike would receive an immediate advance of $2,000 for the car he was planning. I would write another status report for the Institute for America. I noted that we'd received no response from the two I'd sent so far.

It became certain when Jack was talking about the trip down, what we would take, how we would pack the car, how we would divide up the driving, that he had never heard me when I called him. Before I could speak up, Mike quietly noted that I would not be making the trip.

"Of course," said Jack. "I knew it all along. Am I surprised? I was just coming to that." He said I shouldn't worry. The mission was safe in their hands. In fact, he added, he himself had been reluctant, but he couldn't stop thinking about the mission that we'd promised the Institute. He had a vision, he said, of all the children pressing their faces to a chain link fence in the hopes of seeing a real, fire-belching dragster, and the tears that would roll down their cheeks when they realized that they were to be disappointed. He reassured me that he and Mike would make the sacrifice and do what we'd said we would do, no matter how much trouble and inconvenience they would have to endure, or all the extra money they now would have available to spend. They would think of me.

But, hey, as long as you're going to be here anyway, maybe there's one or two things you could take care of while we're toiling in that far distant land.

That's how I found myself at the carwash, walking through it with Mike and Little Mike and taking notes while Mike explained, mostly with his hands, how everything worked, the recurring jobs that had to be done, and where something might break down and what to do when it did. He showed us how he had already done the oiling, adjusting, calibrating, shimming, replacing. Then Little Mike went out to wait on a customer while Mike took me into the storeroom and went over everything there. The day-to-day maintenance – the soaps and the solvents, the belts for the drives. The brooms, mops, and towels; just get the towels over to the laundromat before you run out. On this shelf, spare parts you may need.

In the office he showed me how to run the cash register and then had me show him. Here's the combination to the safe, and here's the key in case you forget it or you mess the combination up and then the safe won't open. On this shelf is the binder with the notes, including the contact information for the suppliers, and the manuals, and the parts catalogs. The refills for the candy machine and the stand for the air fresheners and other accessories are on this shelf; in that corner are the flats of bottles to refill the soda machine. I noticed that the girlie pictures were gone from the walls and that the calendar was now the one from the local funeral parlor.

Should be no problems, he said. He was pretty sure he'd thought of everything, but he'll get me a number for where they would be. Check in once a week. He didn't wish me luck or tell me to stay safe, never asked why I wasn't going, didn't talk about his expectations, just shook my hand, and motored off in his old Jeep to one of his other jobs.

If there was another meeting, I didn't know about it. I was just as glad. I might have had a little flu. I just felt numb. I had felt that way once when I was recovering from a fierce cold. The brain almost stopped working while the body mended itself. Cats are like that. When they were really hurt, they would somehow get to a secure place and shut down while they either recovered or they didn't.

There's hardly any memory of the next week. The memory that does come back is of their departure.

I am standing in the parking lot of the diner. (Was Little Mike there?) Jack lowered the van window to remind me to keep writing to the Institute for America, and I told him that I had and would. Then Jack's battered van pulled out, grumble, grumble, with "St. Guayábe or Bust" whitewashed across the back window, and then the lights of the truck and the white of the writing got smaller and smaller, and then they weren't there at all.

Wake Up, Sleeper

Saturday, November 29

They're gone. Never have gotten used to departures. One minute, there. Next minute, not there. Only the dust in the air, and then even that's lost in the breeze. What happened? Stupid not to accept change, but I don't accept it. It's like that flour sifter of mom's that I keep in the cabinet above the stove. I can clearly see mom using that sifter. It's there, but she's been gone almost fifteen years.

What now? They're gone. Let's do some writing, like we said. Start with the Hal.

Sunday, November 30

Puttered around all afternoon after I got home. Couldn't get organized. Cats seemed to know, they kept wanting attention, both of them. Homily seemed to go okay. Made some Hal notes, write it into here, or write it up separately? Probably already too long, so do a separate draft and then copy it into here? Think about publishing it someday too? One thing at a time, please, sir.

Monday, December 1

Servant heart –

- Be alert. Listen.
- TAKE SOME TIME with Little Mike. Do this!
- Parts catalogs for Mike (does that count?)
- Food to the food pantry?
- Hospital
- Buckhorn this week
- Counsel that couple (find the names, please?)
- Go to Willow Camp? Yes? No?
- Homily: How Blessed We Are

No word from them yet. Shouldn't be surprised. Can't get the weather there either. Did get the weather for November 28 for Havana -- roughly the same? Didn't think about the delay until now

–the only news we ever get here from anywhere in the Caribbean is the weather, and even that's about a week behind.

Made progress with the Hal. So far so good. What to call it? *Hal*? *My Beer Ministry*? Something else?

Tuesday, December 2

Yes! They've arrived.

Long story from Jack about being stopped at the border. Big delay, first because the border is closed on Saturday and Sunday, then a long wait yesterday until there were enough cars and trucks to put together a convoy. They need a convoy for security. It seems there are bandits and insurrectionists in those parts who come down from the mountains and attack lone travelers who travel through this stretch of jungle.

Only, when they finally did get going, there was no jungle near the road, or, if there was, Jack missed it. Still, it took them a full day to go twenty miles, over some mountains and along a big river, through the jungle that wasn't a jungle, surrounded by military patrols and escorts, very impressive uniforms, flags of two nations, jeeps with machine guns and long whip antennas mounted on the back. But they didn't get to see a single bandit. Or maybe they did, said Jack. The fee for the cars in the convoy was 20 bucks American, trucks cost $100. Big discussion over Jack's van. They said it was a truck, Jack said it was a car. They settled for $45. He's sending me a list of all they've spent. "Bunch of pirates," saith Jack, and addeth, "Sounds good so far? Thinking of ya. Call ya tomorrow."

Wednesday, December 3

What first? Well, first, here's the latest news from the Guayávian front. They're settled and rested. Jack said he was disappointed by the house. Thought it would be something colorful: "You know, a hacienda with señoritas to wait on us, big baskets of flowers, masonry arches, a fountain. Not this place, it's a blockhouse, stucco walls and glass brick windows (because of hurricanes, they say), it's like that station KFIC down the road, but at least there's no 200-foot antenna in the back yard here. But everything works, and, what about this phone service? Not bad, eh?" He said I should come, it's almost like home around this place except more houses in this neighborhood.

Mike's already gone to work. Jack dropped him off at the garage where Mike's big boss buddy Frenchy works, the guy he arranged everything through. Some garage! More like a restaurant. Best garage in the world. Everything's spotless. Well-lit, lifts, bays, the whole deal. Working on mostly these pickup trucks, but nothing like we have at home. These pickups are dripping with chrome, big longhorns mounted on the hood, and you wouldn't believe how far up in the air they are. You literally need a stepladder to get into them. Not hauling much fertilizer with those babies. Oh, and also the occasional Mercedes or three. Very nice cars.

That's the good news. Here's the rest of it. You think that palace is where Mike is actually working? No way. Mike won't be there. He'll be off at some hole-in-the-wall shared space in the worst part of town that they set him up with at his request. But that's Mike for you, give him filth and grease and not much light, leave him alone, give him something to do, and he's happy. Jack said he won't be going down there to see this dump, you can bet on that. 'Here's what you have to do, I told him. Go out and see if you can get some local kumquat or two to work with you as a helper. Just do it, and don't sweat the money.'

Jack and Mike haven't made it to this Rosey's place yet. That's tomorrow's plan. Wanted to go, but there was a half-hour wait for the ferry, so got talking to some local clown and ended up taking the tour of the town instead, for only 5 bucks American. Nice place, just like the book said. City of gardens and churches. Beautiful old colonial town square, except for the ultra-modern gleaming totally not colonial hospital across from the courthouse but it's nice to know they have one. Their courthouse is nicer than the one we have in Taylor. Saw the historic cathedral, it's out aways from the center of town and it's a brick-for-brick copy of one in Montgomery, Alabama, where something happened back in the 1860's, something about the Confederacy. By the way, our tour leader was the great-great-grandson of some great Confederate general, didn't catch the name. Otherwise, not as much here about the Old South as we thought there would be, but this local said, Wait 'til Old Confederate Days. That's the eighteenth of February,

I think. And, there is a big market with lots of native stuff, but a little touristy.

So there's today's news from the front. What else? Oh, yes, finished the Hal. Finished the Hal! Be brave, I can do this.

And so to bed. Did read my daily reading, from Paul. With all this writing, don't forget everything else in your life. Be more active. Take a walk. Good to hear Jack's voice.

By the way, here is what I wrote:

Servant Heart

Ever since grade school, they'd called me Preacher, I guess because I seemed to everyone to be quiet and serious and because I had the look. When I got to high school, there was some thought of me going on to a religious vocation. I even thought about it a little myself, but then I got involved with family responsibilities.

Then, when my wife passed away, I still had a child to raise, and a house to run, and a career to support us, but I had time left over that I hadn't had before. I started thinking again about religion, and a calling, and was I meant to be a preacher?

I'd had a pamphlet, called *Servant Heart*, since I was in high school. *Servant Heart* started with a passage in the Bible: *"If any man serve me, let him follow me; and where I am, there shall also my servant be,"* and then went on with an extended meditation on those words. I have to admit that the meditation wasn't of much use to me. It was rich in soaring rhetoric, but mostly lacking in practical application. But it was a vessel for those words of Jesus. Over the years I've often pulled it out, not to read it but just to hold it and hold those words of Jesus.

What would it mean to be a servant of Jesus? Now I had the time to address that question. Basically I've spent most of these years working on that thought.

I soon found out I wasn't much at doing sermons.

Even more, I wasn't attracted in any way to a formal ministry and the sheer administrative burden of managing a congregation. I saw how little time there was for any actual spiritual work when there was so much administration, and fundraising, event planning, personnel and staff issues.

It gradually occurred to me that Jesus and his apostles never had a congregation. Jesus himself couldn't abide the religious establishment of his time. And who *did* he spend his time with? The riff-raff. Tax collectors. Fishermen. Women of dubious reputation. The sick, the lame, the blind. He loved them! And He loved going to parties and weddings , not to preach but just to be there.

So I started doing whatever I could outside the walls of a church. In particular I was helping at our local clinic. It was gratifying and reassuring to know that I could make a difference to people who were suffering, that I could lessen their suffering, but I soon ran into a problem. I was free only at night and on the weekends, and people who need comforting need it at any hour.

Then one day I was over helping old Mr. Polfuss fix the fence by his barn. It was hot; the bandanna around my forehead was soaked, the sweat was beginning to burn into my eyes, and I was thinking that I could really use a short break.

And a cold beer.

Should I really say that? Ask for a cold one?

Then I thought, what is so terrible about a cold beer anyway? Would Jesus have had any trouble with a beer? Jesus certainly liked his wine. He liked being with people, and going to where the people were, the people who really needed Him. And then – my leap – I could do that. I can't do everything the Lord did, or that He calls us to do, but I could certainly enjoy a cold one. And what better place to try that than one of the bars at StateLine? I could sit myself down in a quiet corner, nurse a cold one, and just see if there's something He wants me to do there. Whatever else, it would really take me outside the walls.

Then I thought, is a bar really where they need me most? What about that so-called 'strip club' over on the other side of StateLine? Those poor kids out there have just about every problem that a person could have – trapped, loveless sin, broken families, disease, abuse, drugs, danger.

And then I thought, don't push it, son. Leaping is one thing; leaping over a cliff is another. Don't get too bold too soon. A bar is challenge enough for now. Try it. See what work He has for you there.

So I asked Mr. Polfuss if we could stop for a few minutes, have a short break and maybe even … a cold one. He wiped his sweat off with his shirt, put down his hammer, and exclaimed, Thank the good Lord Almighty, I thought you were never going to stop.

Of course I thought for a while about how to do a beer ministry, and even whether I should, but I couldn't add anything to what I'd already thought, and, after all, if Jesus could, I could at least try. So one quiet day I went over to StateLine, where the two nearest bars were. There was the Buckhorn and Stumpy's, or three if I counted the one in the Dancing Sun Casino, which was run by the Native Nation.

The Dancing Sun Casino was the farthest away. The casino served mainly tourists; it was quite accessible, right on the main highway, a few miles north of the junction where the highway met the road west to Taylor and on up out of the Valley.

As soon as I saw it, I ruled out The Dancing Sun. The bar there was basic, really nothing more than a break area with alcohol. There were no seats in their break area, and no one spent any time there. Obviously most people did their drinking on the gambling floor. When people wanted a break from the machines and the lights, they went right to the adjoining restaurant. I wasn't looking for a restaurant ministry even if I could have figured out a way to do one. Beyond that, the casino was probably the loneliest place I'd ever been. I simply didn't want to be there.

The Buckhorn was at the junction. The Buckhorn was and still is a complex of low, brown stucco buildings that included a gas and diesel station and convenience store, a propane corral, a cabin where truck drivers could wash up, and the combination bar / restaurant. It catered to hunters, farmhands, lumbermen, fire crews, shepherds, and other locals. It had been at the junction since before I was born.

The restaurant there was on one side of a floor to ceiling partition. It was popular; people from the Valley went there regularly. It had the best steaks anywhere for the price. Tourists didn't stop because the place was so dingy; but the regulars all knew each other, and the wait staff and the cooks. Sometimes, after the kitchen closed for the night, the cook would bring out his guitar, and the regulars would sing until the early hours.

The bar on the other side of the floor to ceiling partition was a different place altogether in those days. The people who went there were there to drink. No music, no television, no bright lights, no windows, just people slowly consuming alcohol. On the afternoon I went, there was only a small group, each patron in his or her own space except two men and a woman laughing at the bar, but I knew from the stories the EMT guys told, and from the reports in the *Trumpet,* that the bar was busy on the weekends and that it could occasionally be violent.

I made a mental note to myself to try the Buckhorn some evening and went on to Stumpy's.

I didn't know much about Stumpy's, and I was nervous about what I *had* heard. It had been started only a few years before by outside money to attract an affluent crowd – the summer people -- looking for a 'different' experience. We used to say it was a place where all the doctors, lawyers, engineers, and businessmen could go to a parking lot to compare motorcycles and then go inside to show off their boots and leather jackets. Then it changed. I never really knew how, but the local word was that you did not want to go there anymore. It was still a motorcycle place, but apparently it had gotten rougher.

The afternoon I went there, the parking lot was almost empty. Inside, the bartender was indeed stumpy – my guess was 5'6" and maybe 250 pounds, including the chains, silver stars, the iron cross, and thick waves of tangled black hair. He said the manager was out to lunch, didn't know when he'd get back.

I got a beer and found a booth where I could wait while I inspected the premises. I did not see a place designed for the affluent professional. What I did see was a dance floor, surrounded by booths and lit by neon tubes high up where the walls met the ceiling. Perhaps the space had been remodeled. But how? There was no way one could divide that floor into a more intimate or sophisticated venue, unless they'd created it as a generic space and then constructed their cool and quirky 'experience' to fill it. Or maybe this *was* their idea of a cool and quirky space, which would explain –

"Hi. I'm Hal Stark. You're looking for me?"

I stood up to shake his hand. We sat down, and, after I introduced myself and we talked a bit, I went into my spiel: "Just an idea I had, I'm wondering if I could just come in here and sit for a few hours on some night during the weekend."

"Sure, why not?"

"Wearing my clerical collar."

"You're .. what?"

"Here's what I'm thinking," I said quickly. I explained that I would come in about 9 or 10 on one weekend night, probably

Friday, find a quiet corner, and nurse a beer until around midnight. Wearing my clerical collar. For starters. Be right out front with it. That's all. People could come to me if they wanted to. It was not a problem if they didn't. As to me, I was there to listen, not to talk. I wasn't there to save anyone, or hand out anything, or initiate anything.

I said I realized that no matter how unobtrusive I was, my presence would affect the atmosphere of the place, and proposed that the change might be for the better. It might even make life easier for his bartenders, because there'd be someone else for people to take their troubles to.

I understood it might not work out. If it didn't after a few times, I would quietly pack up and leave, no hard feelings at all. All I was asking was for a couple of hours on a weekend night.

He seemed puzzled. "Could you go over all that again?"

I did. I wasn't going to bother anyone. I wasn't going to try to convert anyone. I was there for anyone who might want to talk. And that was the whole deal.

"Hmm. Let me think it over."

"Can I come back and see you in a few days then, see what you think?" He did not react, so I started for the door. Nice try, I thought. I was really starting to get nervous over the whole scene. I didn't make it to the door.

"Hey."

I went back.

"You're not gonna do nothin'."

I nodded.

"If it don't work out, you'll just go."

Nodded again.

"No hard feelings?"

"No hard feelings."

"Aw, what the hell, why not? Kinky. Are you really a priest? Hey, we get everybody else in here, why not a priest. Sorry about the 'hell,' but you better get used to it, it'll get worse, that's the way we talk around here."

And that's how I met Hal Stark, and the legendary CrazyF***, and the whole gang.

That first Friday night was quiet for me. I knew people were there. Eddies of sound came from the bar, swirls of laughter and loud voices from the booths off to either side, dim forms moving from the door and across the floor, but only the occasional booted feet and denim jeans passing quickly through my small pool of light.

I did have one visitor, briefly. A few minutes after I arrived, a tall, white-shirted, clean shaven young man who I did not know and who was certainly not Stumpy placed a beer silently on the table in front of me and faded into the near darkness. I made a mental note – possible basketball player there – and put a five-dollar bill under the saltshaker.

My glass slowly passed the half-full mark.

After two hours, I finished my glass and turned to pull on my jacket. When I turned back, Hal was sitting across from me. He took the five-dollar bill from under the saltshaker, put it into an envelope he had, and pushed the envelope across the table to me.

"What's this?" I said. I could feel more bills in the envelope.

"You *are* a dumba**, aren't you? What do you think it is?"

"I can't take this." I pushed the envelope back. "I haven't done anything."

"You don't want money? You're a funny priest, aren't you? Try giving it back. Y'know, one of those tens is mine. The beer's on me. I kinda like a quiet night sometimes. See you next Friday?"

"Sure, but there's no need for this. I'm not after anyone's money."

"Listen. Save the story and save up those pennies. Go get yourself a motorcycle jacket. Do you even know what a motorcycle jacket is?"

"I don't know what to say."

"Try, 'Thanks.'"

"Thanks," I said, slowly taking the envelope back. "By the way, about that priest thing. I'm not exactly a priest. It's a long story. A church thing. Technically, if anyone asks, I'm what they call a 'tentmaker,' but I can wear the collar. Which brings me to the other thing. Please, NO publicity. If you ever want to get rid of me, all you need to do is to get my name in the papers. 'Priest Works in Biker Bar.' 'Pastor Has Unusual Ministry.' If that happens, I'm gone. I'll have to be."

"And I can keep that from happening? Sure."

"Well, I don't want any publicity. I get into enough trouble as it is."

"Hey, we all have our secrets here. Let's see how long yours lasts, father. Or padre, or reverend, or rabbi, whatever you are. See you Friday?"

The drive back to Taylor through the pass on the old road takes about an hour. I went that way because I wanted to think. Frankly I hadn't expected any money, and I wasn't sure how to deal with it. Especially since it looked like there might be more envelopes.

By the time I got home, I knew what I wanted to do. Sure, a leather motorcycle jacket sounded like a good idea, but first I would buy the house a round. Figuring 30 people in the bar, that would be somewhere around $200. I would add whatever was needed to whatever was in the envelope and ask Hal to make the announcement.

Figuring out the publicity angle took a little more time. Ultimately Jack and I settled on a story that I hoped would keep things quiet. Word would be that I had committed some unnamed transgression. As a punishment and a penance, so as to atone for my sin, I had to come to the bar and sit for two hours doing nothing,. Until we could come up with a better story, it would have to serve. (We never did, and the problem never came up.)

The next Friday my plan proceeded accordingly. I was cheered and toasted for my generosity, and, as I recall, a couple of people did come over, if only to thank me.

At the end of my evening, there was Hal again, sitting across from me. He pushed an envelope over to me.

"Looks like I'll need to buy a leather jacket. Looks like I'll be able to afford it one of these days."

"Listen, don't get too comfortable. You know I don't think much of your religion."

Probably some of the same things I don't like about it myself, I tried to say, but he went right on without hearing me. "It's just opium for the people. That's what Marx said. And he was some kind of rotten commie. All you're doing is distracting people, taking their minds off their problems. Why don't you actually do some of that good once in a while that you're always talking about in the church?'

"'An opiate for the people,' eh?" I held up my glass of beer and tilted it. "Looks like we might be in the same business."

"Yeah, but this is a bar. They don't come here to be good. They come here to get away from all that," and he was gone. I was disappointed. I wanted to tell him about Jesus and the crowd he chose to hang out with. The Bible actually tells us that. *"The Son of man is come eating and drinking; and ye say, Behold a gluttonous man, and a winebibber, a friend of publicans and sinners!"* I did eventually stop him long enough to quote it as best I could, but he just went into another anti-religion rant. Friend of publicans indeed!

So it went. I wasn't scorned, but I wasn't quite accepted either. Then things changed, and they changed because of CrazyF***.

I had heard about CrazyF****: his rusty flathead motorcycle; his tiny Cushman scooter that he used when his motorcycle wasn't running, which was often; his unique use of the language, his total scorn for personal hygiene.

I learned he was responsible for making Stumpy's what it had become.. It seemed he'd showed up when it was still a gentleman's biker bar, took a look around, snorted, cursed, and proceeded to tear the place apart. He pulled down the bead curtains, smashed the booth partitions with a pool cue, ripped down the art on the wall, and broke all the wine glasses and fine liqueur stock – the Galliano, the Frangelico, the cognacs. No one stopped him; evidently they were all terrified at this tornado that had suddenly wreaked havoc on their little world.

So Stumpy's became a bar where someone like CrazyF*** could come and be accepted, except, as soon became apparent, the legend himself never became acceptable. He was simply too emotionally unpredictable. When he would show up early, he was usually quiet, if a little sullen. Often he brought something to sell that he had made in his machine shop – a plaque, a fine knife, a gunstock inlay. He would answer when people would ask him questions about his work or give advice on some particular technique that he'd used to make the piece he'd brought in.

Other times, particularly late at night, he would show up drunk, belligerent, and, as time went on, increasingly dangerous.

By the time I got there, he was no longer coming to Stumpy's. There were various stories. He'd pulled a knife on someone. He was using drugs. He'd sold drugs on the floor. He had tried to smash a motorcycle that he felt was too dressy. His personal hygiene had become unbearable (I didn't inquire further). He'd gotten into a shouting match with Hal, or with Stumpy behind the bar, or both.

Or he'd just stopped coming because he'd become so antisocial that he wouldn't leave his shop. I preferred that story.

Nevertheless people had affection for him. He was a hero, a person who went beyond all of them in his pure hatred of every convention and every rule, and whose craftsmanship was remarkable. He could be unbearable, but he also could be someone who they wanted to be.

I never actually talked to him. I saw him once. Someone had brought him around. By that time he was in bad shape: a festering cut down the side of his face, scabs, untended hair falling in greasy clumps across his sunken burning eyes, filthy clothes, staggering gait. He hardly noticed the admirers who came up to greet him and share a word or two. He glared around the room. Behind his back, a hat was passed, but when they gave him the collection, he threw it on the floor, cursing loudly and incomprehensively.

Not long after that, he was found comatose in his shop. They got him into the hospital, and he died. That was where I came in. It was assumed that I would be the one to do the service for him. They said, no other minister would refer to him by his preferred name; maybe I would?

Halfway between a joke and a hope.

We gathered at the veteran's cemetery. I'd planned carefully, because I knew that I would; I would use that nickname. I found out his real name, where he'd been born, how he'd learned his skills. In my service I extolled his craftsmanship, his fearlessness, his high professional standards, his surprising sentimentality. When the group gathered about had been brought to the right frame of mind, I used his nickname, the name he was known by. My preparation worked; there were no sniggers, just the handful of women crying and all the men stiff faced, biting their lips.

After that, I was accepted as one of the group. When I would be leaving, there was always an envelope, and sometimes it was stuffed. And the money came right back out again: to help someone with their rent, or a tank of gas, or a pawn to be redeemed. There'd often be something from Hal, usually $10 or sometimes even a $50 bill. 'Business was good tonight,' he'd mutter on those occasions.

Everyone in that place was there because they didn't quite fit in anywhere else, and I was now clearly a person who in my way was a little out of the ordinary too. I had long since stopped wearing the clerical collar, but I still wore something distinctive: sometimes a collarless shirt, and then, more often, a tee shirt with a cross on it. *He may be a preacher, but he's all right*, they said. When I would arrive, Hal would often shout out a greeting: Here's the rev with the opium for the people, or, How's the buzz these days, or, Hope we got us a good stash from the good padre tonight.

I never mixed, never went out on the floor. I stayed in my usual booth. People started coming to me with their stories. Someone put up a crucifix in my booth. I replaced it with the Christian fish symbol, the *ichthys*. Then I started putting out a bowl of breads: sometimes pastries or donuts, sometimes buns and rolls. When people sat down I would offer to break bread with them. I wanted to create a quiet space, and it worked. People didn't come over to party. It got to where I was tied up most of the night, often not leaving until they cut the lights.

To no surprise I learned that the men all had pretty much the same stories: broken marriages, estranged children, legal problems, bad bosses, addiction issues, not enough money, loneliness. The women had their stories too, which were different. Children, yes, but mostly, in that crowd, it was boyfriends, and ex-boyfriends, and loans to boyfriends that were now ex-boyfriends who wouldn't pay the loans back, and unconventional 'business' deals. I was flattered that they shared all their stories without hesitation. None of these stories ever changed much after a while.

One night two women who must have come from the so-called strip club out by the desert, slid into the booth. They were drunk and giggling.

The taller one leaned over confidentially and said, "Y'know, I never made it with a priest before."

"I did. Lots of times," said the other one. "They're just the same as anyone else."

The taller one ignored her and kept talking to me. "You really should try it sometime, father. You don't know what you're missing."

At the bar, Hal was watching. I gave him the nod. It was a signal we'd arranged; it meant, you better come over. As he started, I said to my new friend, "Three things. Thanks anyway, I do appreciate the thought. And, I've been married. And, I'm not a priest."

"Not a priest?" she said. To her friend she said, "Hey, get this, he's not a priest." Hal had arrived. To him she said, "Hey, this guy's not a priest."

"It's a long story," Hal told her. "Actually he's a rabbi."

"No, I'm not," I said.

"What's a rabbi?" the tall one said. "Like a rabbit? You like carrots?"

"Come on, girls, I can get you some carrots at the bar," Hal said, leading them away. As they went, the shorter one said, "I don't care if he's a priest or not, he's kinda cute."

I went back to my beer. Later that night, when I was leaving, I passed the tall one in the parking lot. She was talking with some boys who had a flatbed truck. The driver was leaning out of the window. She was saying, Three of you? In that? For one bottle between all of us? Are you kidding? Aw, go back to your mommies.

The next night, when Hal stopped by with the envelope, he said, You know, you could be helping people like those two. They need you even more than we do. I told him I'd thought about that, but I didn't think I had the skills yet. I'd stick to what I was doing for now, which I thought was better than nothing. He seemed to accept that.

So we settled into a routine. I got to know Hal a little better. At the end of the night, when everything got quieter, we talked.

We often talked about the terminal issues we'd seen play out: ODs, suicides, alcohol poisoning. Lots of ways to kill yourself. Every so often one of them makes it back. Drugs are the worst. Alcohol's not as bad, if you watch your health otherwise. Could I make a point of saying something about health to the people I talked to?

One night I asked him if all his drug talk might get him into trouble. All the stash talk, and the padre with the opium. He said, "I keep it clean on the floor. What they do outside or in the bathrooms, I don't know, and I don't wanna know. If they bust me, they bust me. F*** 'em."

Another night he eased himself into the booth, gave me a long look, and said, "I just don't get you."

"That's all right, I don't always get me either. What's on your mind?"

"You."

I waited. Finally I said, "Me?"

"Yeah, you. I mean, I thought I had people figured. But I can't figure you. I figured that sooner or later you'd start waving that bible around and trying to convert people. Being a real nuisance. And I was really looking forward to the pleasure of throwing you out of here. So what's with you anyway?"

"That's a good question," I agreed, "and I'm not sure how to answer it. Let me try a story." And I told him about my pamphlet, and the words of Jesus, and how I was trying to put those words into practice. I even mentioned Mr. Polfuss, but Hal didn't know him.

Hal listened until I was done, then just shook his head, muttered, I still don't get it, and walked away.

That was about as personal as we ever got.

Until one night.

The weekend before he went on reduced hours for the winter, he hit me with the problem of evil.

Every deacon, priest, minister and anyone else in the religious life gets hit sooner or later with the problem of evil. The problem goes something like this: How can a good and just God have created evil? How come God can't stop evil? Why is there pain and suffering? How could God have allowed the Holocaust?

And of course we have our answers. They're not good answers, because there is no good answer, but we do the best we can. Myself, I have a variety of answers, depending on whom I'm talking to.

I gave one of my better ones to Hal. "Think about a father and a son," I said. "They're partners in a business, a string of tire shops, say. Well, they're having problems with one of the shops. The guys in the shop over there are not sending in their reports. Complaints are coming through about the service and the quality of the tires, and the cost, but they don't answer the phone. They won't talk to the mechanic he sends over there.

"Nothing he can do seems to make the situation any better. Finally he decides to send his kid over to straighten them out.

Surely they'll respect his son. And do you know what happens? They beat the kid up, beat him to a pulp, hang him out bleeding on the fence, and leave him there.

"And the father, who should have known better, was the one who sent him. Why would a father who loves his son do that?"

Hal didn't answer. He seemed choked up. Gee, I'm good tonight, I thought. I went on.

"Well, that father was God, and that son was Jesus. We have a Father who doesn't stop suffering, but who shares it with us, and strenghtens us to withstand it. And in Jesus we have a son who doesn't question the Father, even though he knew exactly what was going to happen to Him. Oh, He tried to talk Him out of it, but He never asked his Father why, never tried to start any deep theological discussion. When the time came, He just did it, did what he was sent to do. That was his Father's will, period. Discussion over. He knew what His Father wanted of Him, and He did it. He was obedient, even unto death."

Hal sat there for a while. It seemed like he was trying to control himself. Finally he spoke.

He was furious. "Get the f*** out of here! Now!"

That was a Friday night. Normally on Saturdays I would go to the Buckhorn if I went anywhere at all. Usually I was home. But that Saturday I went right back to Stumpy's.

I certainly thought about going back. What had happened to make Hal snap? Whatever it was, it was my job to be there, after the story I had told, without worrying about what might happen to me.

I figured, if Jesus could go to the cross, I could risk a broken rib or a few teeth. That's what I told myself. As I arrived, I wasn't so sure. This could really hurt, I thought. *Really* hurt. But look what He went through. If He could go through that, I could do this, whatever it might be.

As soon as I came in, before I even sat down, Hal was hustling toward me, pushing his way across the floor. I was expecting him, and suddenly I shivered. I was afraid.

Almost before that split second ended, I could already see that there was no problem. He was already saying, "Jesus, man, I'm sorry about last night. Can you stay?" That night, after closing, he spent more than an hour with me.

I learned, to no surprise, that he had estranged children, like so many of the other men there. And there was the mommy, and the mommy took the kids, and then she turned the kids against him, and so, f*** 'em all, but they certainly didn't turn the money away, they never stopped wanting more,. Over time, I got to hear what the judge said, how the judge screwed him too, and at the end of the day there's none left to live on, and talk about being screwed, it's all "about the f***ing you get for the f***ing you got!"

One day that spring, Hal mentioned it was his youngest kid's birthday. Sending him a card?, I offered, which was about as much direct advice as I ever gave. Hal offered his usual profanity-filled response.

Then he asked me, "By the way, aren't you the guy whose wife killed herself?"

I could deal with that question. "Not exactly," and for him I added, "And I'm not ready to talk about it." And he dropped it, thankfully.

A few nights later, Hal said to me, completely without emotion, "I sent a card. That card like we talked about? So I got a card back."

"What did it say?"

"Didn't say nothin'. It wasn't from the young one. It was from my oldest." He passed the note to me. It read, 'Thanx for the card, Ron likd it.'

"Now what's next?" I said.

"Now your turn. You spill."

"Still not ready. Sorry."

"I've been spilling my guts, and you're just going to sit there? Thanks, brother." He was disgusted.

"You've got an absolute right," I apologized. "But I can't. Just not ready yet. Feel free to say something colorful."

He glared at me.

I kept apologizing. "It's like I'm asking you to do something that I can't do. Can you do it? Go first? It would help me."

He thought about it, surprised for an instant, then nodded. He was still holding himself in. Finally he muttered, "Know what I'm gonna do?"

"What's that?"

"Gonna send his f***ing momma a card and tell her what the f*** she does with all the f***ing money I send her. F***ing a**, she could f***ing teach the f***ing kid how to f***ing spell, is f***ing what! Even I f***ing spell better than that. And who am I but just some dumba**, the dumbest f***ing a****** that ever dumped his f***ing a** onto a f***ing scoot!"

As time went on, he let me talk more. I talked about forgiveness. Said a little about acceptance. All the while I wondered what right I had to preach to him at that point, but he listened. And I wondered when and how I would ever come through with my promise to him.

A few weeks later, he came to me. "Sent them a card. Said 'Happy Easter.' Me! 'Happy Easter.' With glitter on the letters. Wanted to write, 'Go fornicate yourselves, all of you', but I wasn't sure how to spell it. Wanted to write, With love from dad. Didn't do that either. Just wrote, 'Dad.' Next time it'll be rabbits and little duckies! And as to you. You know what you can go do to yourself too."

So it went. He was working and reporting back. One day he told me he got a call from his son. The oldest one again, the other two still weren't ready to talk to him. And then, after another few weeks, they'd met. Not much had happened, it wasn't comfortable, but they'd met. The son looked like him.

Time passed. And then his son called him, wanted to come to him for advice. Joining the Marines might be a future, but first he wanted to know what his father thought. Funny about that, Hal told him, I was just doing some thinking myself. Thinking about selling this place and opening a tire shop down your way. I know this guy who's retiring. Whaddya think?

Then I didn't see him at Stumpy's anymore. His son lived down below, and Hal moved down there. Once he left, the place started to get a little rougher, and I started finding reasons to go to the Buckhorn instead. A year or so later I read that the police had shut the place down. (I'd gotten several calls not to go there that night. I'd hardly been there in months, but evidently my callers just wanted to be sure.) The story said that the officers, who were assigned from several jurisdictions, had observed drug dealing, drug use, underage drinking, and prescribed public sexual acts. They had confiscated weapons, motorcycles reported as stolen, and drugs and drug paraphernalia.

Even though it reopened the next week, that was the end of Stumpy's; too many of their patrons were behind other bars. Since then it's been a meditation center, a megachurch, and a private school. These days it's an indoor flea market and apparently doing quite well.

As to me, I found a welcome at the Buckhorn, which has become a much quieter place. They tell me that the guys who used to come there for a fight are now going to a place up by Sadler.

I did see Hal again after that. One morning Mike, Jack, and I were coming out of the diner and he was coming in. He was with a young man who looked like him a lot. He started to say, I would like you to meet my – but that was as far as he got before his face got tight. So did mine. So did his son's. There was no way I could introduce them to Mike and Jack without cracking up, so I let them go with a nod and hustled Hal and his son back into the diner where I had another breakfast, and they had their first on the day, and we were all able to talk a little.

Later, Mike and Jack were embarrassed but respectful. Actually Mike was respectful, and Jack was embarrassed. I told them what they needed to know. I told them I felt totally good about what had happened. Men have feelings too, or so it's said.

Thursday, December 4

Well, there's a load off. Now let's see if I can keep this going.

Cloudy and cool early, then warm, then almost chilly in the evening. Winter holding off so far.

Found many important things to do.

Stopped off at the car wash. Not much money in the till, won't be as long as the weather stays dry. Little Mike said they had one truck that was so muddy he had to run it through twice.

Something wrong with Mildred? She was crying and wouldn't leave my lap when I was reading the paper. At the gym, couldn't hit my threes at all, so worked with the kids and then went and did a few laps and my stretches and then came back but still couldn't hit a three. Hope I don't hit a tree.

And so on to today's report from the land of sand and palms. All Jack wanted to talk about was Rosey's place. Jack was speechless. He was so overwhelmed that he didn't know where to start. Mere words could not describe this place of Rosey's, I need to drop everything, get my ticket, and come down and see for myself. I need to be the one to write this place up and do it justice.

Well, knowing my man, I started him with just one thought. Tell me more about this Rosey. That was all it took to get him started. This Rosey is unbelievable. You have to see this guy. You've never seen anyone like him. Definitely not from our neck of the woods.

Then the connection went bad and didn't come back. Tomorrow I'll get the full story about Rosey and his wonderful establishment?

Friday, December 5

Turns out the phone problem is on the East End only. Phones are even working in town, just not along here. A crew is working down the road. Still have power, thankfully.

Too much happening. Starting to wonder if I'll get it done, or if I'll just drop the ball.

Found a folder from the library that I'd missed because it was buried under some newspapers, and found this in it:

> 'Rosey' Poitier Says Hello
>
> At 6'3" and 305 pounds, Roosevelt 'Rosey' Poitier may not have been the biggest tackle on the Bearcat line during the Marchmont years, but he was their biggest character. "You always knew where Rosey was," recalls Coach Marchmont, "but he sure made some big plays for us." Who can forget the playoff contest against the Grizzlies, when he sacked the opposing quarterbacks three times and led the charge that stopped the Grizzlies cold just yards from the goal line in the dying moments of the game.
>
> Noted for his heads-up play, enthusiasm, and leadership on the field, his greatest contribution may have been in the clubhouse. His infectious high spirits could be counted on to cheer a discouraged teammate or remind an overenthusiastic rookie to 'cool his jets.' A teammate recalls, "He was always singing. He could

make up songs just like that, and he had a way of getting a necessary point across with a little ditty when words might just have made things worse."

Although 'Rosey' was born in Westchester County, New York, his roots are in the Caribbean. His father, a successful artist, came from the tiny Caribbean nation of St. Guayábe. His mother worked for the company that made the very fashionable "White Nights" line of lingerie. Originally a dancer from the famed Novgorod Ballet Company, she fled Russian persecution via Paris before coming to the United States. A little-known fact about Rosey is that he is fluent in both Russian and Yiddish.

An All-State in his high school years, Poitier was a much-feared pass rusher at Northern State until drafted into pro ball after his junior year. When injuries ended his six-year pro career, he had a short stint as a sports broadcaster before going into the hospitality industry. Today Rosey and wife Katrina Ivanova run a successful business and restaurant in his father's native St. Guayábe.

He misses his Bearcat teammates and plans to attend this year's team reunion. Hope you make it, Rosey!

Side job next week. The summerhouse windows are in, I can pick them up Monday morning. Too many windows! Now, off on my bar run. Hope Jack remembers I'm not always around on a Friday night. That is, if the phones are even working.

Oh, and found a note in my mailbox from the high school. They want to know if I can come in sometime next week for an hour and talk to the journalism class about common grammatical errors. Sending back the following:

I'm happy to be invite but must remind you of my lack of recent experience and also I'm not prepared, with all it's many demands, its not easy to jest step in. I would love to be their, but you have the write to respect all of you're colleagues to have the full set of skills to work with, Not some poorly part-time armature like me." Because, Poor Teaching is a problem for every body. However, in the last analyst I guess if your asking me so you know all that and you want me anyway so it all jest completely centers around me simply being they're and do what I can do, which I'll try to be.

Saturday, December 6

Seemed like a fight brewing at the Buckhorn, so I left early, hoping the phones worked and Jack would call. And he did, called a little after midnight, very excited. He has a job for me back here. Seems he was talking business with Rosey. Seems Rosey's little establishment isn't exactly what it seems. Wait until I hear the story, and then he has a little job for me.

Get this, saith he. He's talked to Rosey. Really talked. They're buddy-buddies now, he calls Rosey 'Squeaky,' and Rosey calls him 'Jackson Hots.' Anyway, this Rosey's not your average kumquat. Haven't seen him do a lick of work around here yet. Like he says, all he does is just wander around the tables with this big floppy flowery hat and cutoff khakis and sandals, and play his songs on the ukulele, act colorful, keep everybody happy, and end every other sentence with 'mon.' And smile. Like his wife says, always to smile.

He has some kids working the bar, and he sings to them and talks to them just like they were customers when he's not posing for pictures and signing autographs. And if there's no one working the bar, you can go make your own drinks and just pay for them yourself, you leave your money in this pirates' treasure chest.

All the heavy lifting is done by these kumquats at the bar that they hire off the street. And his wife. She does the ordering and the hiring and firing, and keeps the books. You know she was a stewardess on Aeroflot? That's the Russian airline? She says they used to tell all the stewardesses that, with Americans, you smile; all the time, smile. And Rosey's mother was from Russia too? Big in lingerie or perfumes, something like that.

So she works, he smiles and 'mon's,' and it's all good for ol' Rosey and the missus.

You think this is a real happy little scene? Some little shack on the beach, peddling the exotic potable to the wandering weary traveler? Lemme tell you, as a businessman I maybe notice things that other folks may not, and what I see is a moneymaker.

The bar covers his expenses. Even his 'payments.' But there's more. Like, the ferry service is his, and he gets a cut on the anchorages.

And then there's the real money. It's the stuff he sells. He could run the bar for free just to have a place for all the stuff he sells. He's got his tee shirts and pens and jewelry, hot sauces and beach balls, postcards, decorative paddles, cozies and coasters, books, custom ukuleles, songbooks and recordings. He has pictures of himself and his ukulele that he autographs.

He's got this signature drink, the Pirate's Revenge, and you can buy a dry mix with recipe to take home, and he sells this crazy hat with a pitcher built into it and a hose with a spigot so you could tap it for a little pick-me-up, any old thing to help you make it through this cruel, harsh world.

He even as an island Santa bobblehead doll that brings in ten grand a year all by itself, and it talks -- says "Merry Christmas, mon!" And it's all branded with his Rosey's World Peace and Love Shack name. Counting the store at the airport and the mail order business, he nets over two hundred grand a year.

But get this. He also sells something called *chachkes*, and he gets another two hundred grand from those. And so here's what I'm saying. No reason at all why *we* couldn't have those 'chachkes' too.

So, listen, here's what I need you to do for me. Go find out what these 'chachkes' are and get back to me. Start small with these chachkes things. Just price out a few boxes or however they come. Once people figure out what to do with them, that's when we'll go big. And this all could be good for you too. I'm thinking, if I get too deep into the tee-shirts – people will want ' Jack's Car Wash' tee-shirts --- and all the rest of that stuff, you could take over the whole 'chachkes' side, and we'll split 50-50. Whaddya think?

I told him I'd get right on it first thing Monday morning.

I keep forgetting that I need to find out more about Mike's cars –something when I write the Institute. Talk to Mike!

And then to bed, totally done.

Also, should send the first of the Carolyn stuff off to Hal soon. Will I? Scary, but I was right; it's time. Sent this note off to Hal today. Serves him right.

Hey, Hal,

Wonderful seeing you and your son at the diner too long ago. Praying things also work out with the other boys.

Guessing it's my turn now to do something. Soon I'm going to send you a few words about *my* situation. My wife, I mean, that we talked a little about. And it won't be a few words, I've already got a few pages. Thanks for being patient with me, and my too few words up to now about her; I promise I'll make up for it! Forgive me if I get a little long-winded. Remember how much I didn't want to talk about her and how hard I tried to spare you! In a few days I'll check in with you, see what you think of what I've sent so far, and see if you want to read more. If you don't, I understand. Until then,

Your friend,
Jim

Now, go to bed, goose.

Sunday, December 7

Up early to help raise the flag at City Hall. Fewer people again this year. Some old-timers – Mr. Polfuss, Artie Stryker -- did come in their uniforms. Wondering how they felt; they certainly looked proud.

Then spread the homily around town: How Blessed We Are. Home for late lunch, wrote all afternoon, and that was my day. Down to Erin's Monday? Mabel her usual self, Mildred superb on her perch.

Monday, December 8

Servant heart --

- Take the time. Don't hurry. Respect the tools
- Start on hams for food pantry
- Check trash cleanup at the park and Willow Camp
- Hospital
- Casino this week? (meteor shower?)
- Get last year's budget from the county clerk
- More Carolyn
- Homily: Preparing Our Hearts

- Talk to Martin this week?

And don't forget the Institute!

Actually .. do forget about the Institute. Keep writing the reports, because the reports make a good way of keeping track of what we've done and what we plan to do next. And then send the reports off, because why not? Costs only a stamp, and who knows? But I can't believe we'll ever hear from them again.

Can't see Erin this week, I'll have the garden summerhouse job to finish after work. Where's my head these days? Toooo much going on. Too many people in my heart. So get some work done tomorrow, please, Mr. James.

Little Mike called; he's not going in today. It's slow anyway, and I've got enough to do, so decided to close it down. Hope he makes it tomorrow. Or else, what? Can't stay closed for too long, even if the snows haven't started yet. Maybe my turn to put the shoulder to the wheel?

A cricket under the stove this morning, loud and strong. He found his way in, but can't find his way out.

Phoned over to the library to ask them to find out what they could about *chachkes*. She'll see what she can do, and will call back probably tomorrow.

Took delivery on the windows; everything looked okay so far.

No word from St. Guayábe for a change. Waiting on me?

And heeere we go:

Those Memories ..

Short story. I loved her, I lost her. It's been twenty years since, and so far I really haven't moved on. Maybe it's time to let go. Maybe, right? Writing may help. Here goes.

I don't remember a time that I did not know Carolyn Gaertner. We were pushed together early. She was an only child, and so was I. We were both quiet but approachable. From the beginning we were both tall for our age and athletic.

My folks and hers, the Gaertners, were neighbors. All of them were on the same bowling team for years and went to the same church. The Gaertners had the house at the corner of Buena Vista and Resaca, and we were two doors down on Buena Vista.

We grew up together. They had a sandbox; my earliest memories of Carolyn are of taking turns moving sand around with my old yellow metal steam shovel (I still have it) and her not wanting to give it back until I said the 'magic word.' I can still see her in the sandbox, mud and sand all over her face, and smiling angelically.

Every few months the newspaper would have some kiddie picture, and half the time Carolyn would be it: petting a lamb or making faces at a pig, opening a present, wearing a witch's hat at Halloween, helping to rake leaves, selling cookies or lemonade, playing with a garden hose or running through a lawn sprinkler.

As we got older, she had all the board games with all the pieces, and the little interlocking bricks and the logs, and we didn't, so we played a lot at her house, particularly in the winter.

We loved the movies. You didn't have to cross the street to get from her house to the theater – the Variety, do you remember it? It's where the Bistro Nouvelle is now – so we must have started to go see movies together when we were about six, and we kept right on going until we were teenagers and the movies had gone from black and white to color – Technicolor! – and from cowboy sagas and outer space serials to big stars and musical romances.

I especially remember the outer space movies, how the rocket ships glided across the screen and you could see the guide wires, or how you could see the string pulling the rocket ship up when it blasted off. When we'd get back to her house, she would be Princess Falala the Magnificent, and I would be Dale Dawson, Intergalactic Explorer, and she would beg to save me from the king's wrath after I had accidentally trespassed into the Sacred Vestibule of the Ancient Ones.

By that time we were in grade school. We were both good students, but there was something special about her in school. Teachers adored her. She never seemed to work at anything, yet she always got good grades. She was friends with everyone. Every year she was the madonna in the Christmas pageant.

At recess, she was always one of the first ones chosen, because she was one of the best pitchers in the schoolyard when she wasn't playing shortstop (or even quarterback on the football team). It never bothered anyone on her team that she was a girl, even though she used to set her dolls next to the pitching mound so they wouldn't get lonely on the sidelines while she was out there striking out the other side.

Of course all that changed when we got to middle school. We had to stop eating lunch together. She wasn't allowed to play sports anymore. The boys played over here, and the girls played over there, and the teachers made sure that it stayed that way. Looking back, I can understand why, but back then I remember being puzzled and annoyed for a year or two, until Mother Nature started to go to work on us. Then I understood. As to Carolyn, she just went right on – first as cheerleader, then head of the cheerleading squad.

After school we would have cookies and milk in her kitchen and giggle over what we had seen that day, and then do homework together or listen to records.

By that time she had the most amazing walk. When she walked, she seemed to be floating on air. All of us would stop in the halls or on the street to watch her, kids and grownups alike. She was a queen now, and she knew it, but her walk said it was no big deal to her; that was just the way things were and always had been. I know her, we're friends, I wanted to say to anyone else standing there as she went by. We're friends.

As high school approached, we became a little distant. I don't recall whether that was me or her or both of us. From my side, somehow it was wrong to have a girl as one of your best friends. It wasn't 'cool.' Mom said that people might wonder about me, or us, whatever that meant. And I did want to be 'cool.' What might happen if I weren't?

Then she moved. In that summer, the last summer before high school, the Gaertners left Taylor. A corporation down below had bought out her dad's grocery store and moved him to corporate regional headquarters.

A year later she and her mother were back, without her father. Something had changed in her. Maybe it was the family breakup, or maybe it was just growing up. They still had their house, but the milk and cookies in the kitchen was all over. All that autumn we wordlessly made a point of avoiding each other. In the classroom we sat on opposite sides of the room.

When we did meet by accident, she said hello and smiled. Once her mother invited me and my parents to have dinner with them. At dinner, if her mother was hoping that some spark between us would ignite, it didn't. I guessed her mother might be worried about her, but, whenever I did see her, at school or at the drive-in, she was always with a group of the girls.

We did have one short time together. Even though we were both only sophomores, she was chosen to be the Queen of Winter at the Harvest Pageant. I was the only boy in school who was both taller than she was *and* able to remember lines, so they asked me to try out to be her Consort. The rehearsal did not go well. I felt I wasn't that bad, but she had problems. She dropped lines, seemed confused. Halfway through the tryout, the director called a halt, talked with her briefly in private, and then said I could go home.

I was just going out the door when she caught up with me. She apologized for what had happened and asked me to call her the next night.

That was when we started to talk.

We still were hardly seen together, but she called me every week or two for the rest of that sophomore year. At first the calls were simple. She left her geo textbook at school, could she borrow mine until tomorrow? Did I have a copy of the new record that the girls were talking about in the locker room? Her mother was at work, could my father and I take her for a quick trip downtown to buy milk?

Gradually I really got to know her again. We talked more. I soon learned something that no one else seemed to know about her.

Her life was a mess. Boys were uncomfortable talking to her. She'd hardly ever been out on a date, and never with the same boy twice. She never felt she was one of the girls. Her mother was angry and drinking too much. She missed her father a lot, though his phone calls helped some. She was everyone's friend, and no one's.

I remember asking her if she wanted to have friends. She was so lovely, and she was so lonely.

"Of course," she said. "Doesn't everyone?"

"But what do *you* want?"

"I just want to be like everyone else."

In those days I was just learning to talk and listen. I was afraid of saying the wrong thing, of hurting someone. So I dropped it at that point, but I went to dad and told him what was happening and what she'd been saying.

He said, "What are you getting out of this, Mr. James?" Dad was always after me to be mature and responsible, and calling me 'Mr. James' was one way he had of making his point.

"I want my friend to be happy."

He nodded. We talked over a few ideas, which ended up that he would call her father and I would advise Carolyn to see if she could get an idea of where she wanted to go in her life, a goal, so that she could start taking one step at a time toward that goal. First and most of all, she just needed to settle herself down, take herself in hand, get a *grip* on herself.

I didn't know what he meant by that, but dad was emphatic: she needed to get a *grip* on herself.

The next time I talked to her, I did my part. She heard me out, thought about it, said, "Good point. Seriously. But I don't know what I want. Besides a life. I know I don't want what I have now. I want something different."

Dad must have done his part, because the next weekend her father was in town to take her shopping for a car.

That's when she did something surprising. With his money, they could have bought any car at any dealer, but she fell in love with an ancient roadster in the back row of one of the lots. Dad said it reminded him of the cars they had when he was young. It was like a 'flivver," he said, so we all started calling it "Da Flivver."

The car needed work. That car always needed work. It would break down constantly, and she would have to hike to some nearby house and call for help. I was always a little nervous about that, but she was delighted with her various adventures.

In a way that car was how my friend Mike Charney really got started as a mechanic. (You might remember Mike; that was him and my other great friend, Jack Van Dorn, that you met at the diner.) In those days he was just helping out around Mr. Carson's garage, but Carolyn wanted him to be the one working on her car, so Mr. Carson had one of the mechanics show him the simple maintenance routine, and Mike just went on from there.

So the three of us started spending time together. I remember one time we were making a test drive after his latest repair, all of us jammed in the front seat.

Where do you want to go?

I don't know. Where do you want to go?

We found ourselves at the pond by the willow grove; Willow Camp, if you know it. A pair of swans had taken up residence in the pond. 'Going to see the swans' was the big entertainment in Taylor that fall. People still say that around here sometimes, although now it has a different meaning, or maybe it did even then. We stood at the edge of the pond and watched one of the swans glide effortlessly across the water, serene and unattainable.

I said, "That's you. You're a swan."

"You think so? Well, easy for you to say, you're a goose, a silly goose, like you've always been ('goose' was one of her childhood nicknames for me), and you," to Mike, 'what are you? What's that face? You're the grumpyduck?"

Mike answered, "It's not that, it's just I really got to be getting back. A lot of work back at the shop." (That was in the days when Mike still talked, before he decided there was already too much talk in the world.)

It was on the way home, I think, that we made up one of our songs, to the tune of *Suwannee River*, and I still remember it:

Two Dogs in Goose and Swannie's Flivver
Arf, arf away!

Not sure how the dogs got into it, because Carolyn and I were both cat people, but 'Meow, meow away!' just doesn't work in the song. Mike always had dogs, so they might have been his contribution, or maybe me and Mike ourselves were the dogs.

When her car finally had its terminal breakdown, we wanted to push it next to dad's old Ford behind the garage, but he said no, one old piece of junk was enough. She went without a car of her own for a month or so, until her dad could get back to the Valley, but it didn't matter as much, because Mike and I had a car that we were sharing until we could each afford a car of our own.

We still did things together although not on campus. We had been playing pickup basketball games in the gym with whoever showed up until the whispers started that a girl shouldn't be playing in the same games with the boys at school, so we moved the game to the court at the town park until the police came and stopped us. It was for our own good, they told us. Girls were too delicate to play boy sports. If she got hurt, someone was going to be in real trouble, and, you know, nobody wants trouble. So we stopped, which was a shame because she could still throw and shoot as well as we could, and she was quicker than Mike.

At school she seemed happier. The late-night phone calls almost stopped. She was enjoying cheerleading, although she told me she had to keep her moves simple so that the other girls could follow her. Maybe the other girls were otherwise occupied; according to my friend Jack Van Dorn, and I believed him, Carolyn was the only virgin left in our class.

After junior year, she was sent away to some girls' finishing school near Chicago for summer session. When she came back, she was much more grown-up. Our play days were indeed finished. Instead of phone calls and outings, she wanted to go to the dances and events. Mike was the one who escorted her. Frankly, I was quite content to let Mike have her all to himself for those occasions. I had no problem avoiding the dances and shows altogether. Those days I was busy with a sudden passion for music, listening to and trying to play Bartok or Strindberg on mom's piano.

On a date, she wasn't much fun, Mike told me. It seemed that she could dress up like a grownup, make the approved gestures and speak in a proper tone of voice. At the dances and the events, she made a fine appearance, but she wasn't comfortable. In a group, she had no small talk at all. Knowing Mike's skills as a conversationalist, even back when he was still talking, I used to wonder if they spoke three words to each other in a whole evening.

And it wasn't working out for Mike. He *was* looking for what we used to call 'fun.' She wasn't it, but he was a good sport and kept up his end for the first few weeks of our senior year, until he started getting mixed up with a Diane (or was it Sandra?), but that's a story for another time.

About the time that Mike moved on, she called me again. I wasn't completely surprised, because we were still friends, but I was getting serious about basketball then and she was now a grownup.

I don't remember the beginning of the conversation much, until she said, out of the blue, I don't think the other girls like me. She said, I envy you so much. You have Mike and that Jack and all your other friends. (She never cared for Jack and would have nothing to do with him.)

We talked for at least an hour. Where my parents were, I don't remember, but I remember just about everything Carolyn said from that point on. Was her smile truly sincere when she said hello to the other girls? Did she really care when she said, 'How are you?', or was she just being proper? Did she stand up quickly enough when she stood up in class? Or was she too quick? She wanted to be 'proper.' She wanted to be 'good,'

She was particularly concerned about how she was, how she behaved, with Theresa. Theresa was the only Indian on the cheerleading squad and one of the few Indians in the whole school. And Carolyn couldn't deal with it. Was she being right with Theresa? Was she treating her just the same as every other girl on the squad? Or should she do more to defend her and support her? Should she take Theresa under her wing? But what did that mean? And would that be doing too much? Would that be patronizing? And did she really love and respect and truly, actually, care for Theresa, or was she only doing what she thought she was supposed to do?

By this time she was starting to break down. As she went on, she kept having a harder time talking, almost choking as she tried to get the words out. She finally broke down. Really, she said, is that my whole life now, just a show? Just a performance? And who am I really? And how do I find out? And where do I go from here? And how did I lose it so totally?

At that moment, I tell you my heart went out to her. I had never cared so much for anyone as I cared for her at that moment.

I have never forgotten how I felt that night, or all the occasions since then when that same feeling has swept over and into me. The feeling had nothing to do with passion. I did not feel any differently about her as a person exactly. The feeling was not so much about her as an individual as it was about the totality of life as I knew it.

At first it felt like a feeling about itself. Then it became a feeling about all the feeling in the whole world. I remember thinking about all the need in the world. We in the Valley had our homes, parents, education, decent clothes. So many of the people in the world don't. If *we* could suffer, how could they endure?

And there was not just the suffering, but all the feelings. It seemed that the more we entered into life, the more overwhelming life became, as if suddenly a person in a dark, closed room had opened the shades and was stunned, knocked flat, by the intensity of the sun.

So I had that piece, the 'needs of the world' piece. What I didn't have then, and have slowly been gaining since, is the other piece – that there was so little I could do about that suffering and those needs, but, nevertheless, if I meant to follow Him, to be His servant, that meant that I was to use all my strength and all my abilities to do whatever I could and leave the outcome in His hands.

That's not quite it, but I think that words only go so far. Anyone who has had that feeling already knows what I'm trying to describe, and anyone who hasn't had the feeling won't know until they do.

After that, we talked as much as we could, almost every night. She simply had to try to talk her pain away, and I was hungry for that feeling again, that burning endless caring. Neither of us could stop. Out of habit we stayed polite and distant in public for a while, but then we started eating lunch together. Neither of us really cared at that point all that much if people did find out how together we were.

At first she did most of the talking. She talked, I listened. Nothing I could think of to say had much effect, but, when we started sharing hugs, the hugs seemed to comfort her. She started calling me 'big brother,' and I was calling her 'big sister,' but she wanted me to call her just 'sister,' so I did.

Then she didn't want to take the chance of being seen crying in public, so when people were around I started doing more of the talking. That also seemed to help. When I talked, she could go back to what she was supposed to be: kind, supportive, gently comforting. Looking back, I wonder if I helped at all. Probably nothing would have helped, but at least she was able to gain some control over herself.

I should add, I was happy to have the chance to talk as well. There were some decisions I needed to make.

In those days I was very nervous about college. My mother expected me to go to seminary. Dad thought a regular college would be better for me, but was very quiet about it. We really didn't have the money for either -- hardly anyone did where we were. There were correspondence institutions of both types that we could (barely) afford, but we felt and everyone said that people should go away for college if there was any way to do it.

Was seminary my future? The work seemed demanding, but I would come out with a job that was, if not lucrative, at least dependable and in line with the values I was raised with. It seemed that there was money available if I wanted to go in that direction, but nothing seemed sure. Anyway, money was not my biggest problem. My real problem was that, even then, I wondered if I could do it. I'd watched very carefully to see what ministers actually did during their day, and let's skip the miserable details and just say that I wondered if it was something I could ever do. Maybe I had too much esteem for the clergy, but I didn't want to insult their service by just going through the motions myself. I needed to find another way that was my own.

When I was a junior, I realized that, if I wanted to go to a regular college, I was going to need an athletic scholarship, so I got serious about the basketball. I needed to be concentrating totally on my game instead of me and Carolyn being on the phone or sitting out in the car in the boonies for hours. She envied me because I had the basketball experience in my life, but was clearly troubled at the thought of us spending less time together and then me going away in less than two years.

I started really putting myself into my game, and, by the time I was a senior, my game was showing it. That final year of basketball was a story unto itself, which I may get into yet. Suffice it to say that it went very well, as well as it could have. Somehow, I'd gained the ability to focus. When I put the ball up, it went in. When the other team had the ball, I knew where to go and what to do. Almost without thinking, I was directing the other guys on the floor. Sometimes I felt I was even directing the other team. It was turning into a good year. I had hopes.

One day the coach pulled me aside. He had made a call to an old teammate who was now an assistant coach at a big Midwestern school. I was not to repeat our conversation to anyone. He was confident that, if things worked out, I might get a real offer there. Maybe, just maybe, a dream package: tuition, books and fees, housing, a part-time job. But it would take a real commitment from me. Keep my focus. Keep my intensity. Just winning wasn't enough. Our league was too small, it wouldn't work as a showcase. We needed a bigger stage, and, to get there, I needed to do more. If I could, he thought he could get us an invitation to the Regionals.

Of course I immediately got on the phone to Carolyn. That night we were out behind dad's garage, sitting in that old Ford that dad had been planning to rebuild one day when he retired. I controlled my excitement. In my best calm, everyday voice, I told her about my possibilities. In her same voice she told me she was pregnant.

Tuesday, December 9

Cricket still under the stove. Another cricket outside. It seemed like they were calling each other, back and forth. Thought about them all day. Do crickets mate for life?

Got a call from the library late. Jack's not going to be happy. "Chachkes" is just a Jewish word that means 'little knick-knacks.' In other words, those mugs, tee-shirts, and all that *are* chachkeses.

There's no separate things that are chachkeses. Oh, well, there goes my golden future. Thanked her and asked if she could find out about crickets, no hurry.

Wednesday, December 10

Call last night from Jack. Long story about this person at Rosey's who does animal impressions. He says she must be some kind of local legend. Here's the deal: Rosey rings this big brass bell and everyone starts shouting, Amanda! Amanda! So this skinny broad comes out, bows to the crowd. Not much to look at. Weird hair, kind of straight on one side and curly on the other. Blondie.

"So, after she finishes her shy smiley bowing thing, she says, 'Tonight we will meet a great traveler, the sea turtle. The sea turtle is such a remarkable animal. The lady turtle comes from miles away one night a year to lay her eggs in the sand and then goes away, never to return. And when she swims, she looks like this.'

"So then this broad fills her cheeks with air and then releases it, fills up again, and all the time she's popping her eyes open and closed. The audience is howling. She's great. She really is a turtle. Then she flops down and crawls along the beach almost like she's swimming, digs a hole in the sand and then fills it in again, patting down the sand. Then she stands up, blows a kiss to the mound and backs away slowly. And then she like swims away forever, and she stops every few steps to turn and wave goodbye. Just before she disappears in the darkness she says, 'And this is the story of the sea turtle. Thank you so very much. Please come back next week, when we will meet the amusing and amazing pelican.'

"So I go up to her afterwards and tell her I'm a big Hollywood agent and I think I can get her some work. Just making a big joke of it, you know, but she believes me, she's all excited. Hold on, I think to myself, better come clean. So I ask her about herself instead, and I get a long story, how she's a Yoga instructor and has a studio in town, or wants a studio in town, and she's here because she hopes she can meet someone who can share her dream, someone who can help her build her future. Ho, ho, says I, and wish her good luck and beat it out of there. I like broads and I like money, but don't ever put them together, is what old Jack says."

And with that he was gone. Still want to tell him about the car wash, just let him know how things were going, but he never asked. He hasn't asked yet. And Mike, how's he doing? I did tell him about the chachkeses. Hey, we tried, he said.

Oh, and Hal. Wrote this:

Hal,

Hope you had the chance to read my story up to now, and, if you didn't, I understand. This thing looks like it will go on for a while, and you may already have heard all you want or need to hear. Please give me a call if you want more. This thing is not easy to write. Without you to write it to, I don't know if I'll do it, but it's starting to look like I will, no matter what. If you just want the rest of it short and sweet, I'll be happy to do that too. Please let me know.

Your friend,

Jim

And so to bed.

Thursday, December 11

Not only do crickets not mate for life, but it seems the lady cricket maintains a lifestyle that would be condemned from every cricket pulpit if they had them. Enough said.

Thinking on 1 Peter 3:18-19. Did Jesus really go to hell and preach to the people there after his crucifixion and before his resurrection? And not all the people, but only the people who didn't make it onto the ark in Noah's time? Does that mean that the people in hell or some of them still have a chance for redemption, that God has not forgotten or forsaken them? Very nice to think so.

And how does Peter know this? Did he or the people around him come up with the story? *Or did Jesus himself tell this to Peter?* Are these actual words from Jesus that are not in the Gospels?

Pulled a few of my commentaries off the shelf to see what they had to say, found a lot of words and speculation and even distortion of the text, but it didn't sound like they knew any more than anyone else. Really, why should they? A text to ponder, but not enough there to reach any conclusions. Another question to ask Him when.

There are times I wish I'd listened to my mother and gotten a proper religious education.

Drove by the car wash. Doors were open. Little Mike must have been inside, his bicycle was there, but no customers.

Got a call from Morrie. He had a major breaking story and needed about 150 words and a picture *soonest*:

Jim Lawrence
11 December
154 words
(Photo by Jim Lawrence)
Gym Repairs Underway

The long-awaited repairs to the windows and roof of the gym clerestory have begun. The major holdup was the availability of a crane of sufficient height to do the work, but, after many adventures, the required item is in place and working.

Local dignitaries and a largish crowd of students and other Taylorites gathered on December 11 to watch the crew set up the crane. In the picture above, County Supervisor Randy Grisman, County Engineer George Booth, Mayor Jack Clark, and coaches Sherri Walton (women's) and Rob Grassley (men's) welcome Construction Foreman Samuel Saltzer to Taylor.

The crane partially visible in the background is a Syracuse Jupiter 440, with 16" x 24" cylinders and 5' driving wheels. It weighs 65,450 lbs. and develops approximately 11,500 pounds of tractive effort. Word is that the work will take about two weeks to complete, so hurry if you want to see this mechanical marvel in operation.

[Friday, December 12 - no entry]

.. Of You ..

Old Fords smell different. This one always smelled like a bear had been hibernating in it. Maybe a leak here, and a one-time family of squirrels there; we never did figure out the source. Add in the odor of the cracked leather seat, the horsehair stuffing under the seats, and dust, all mixed together. I let myself dwell on all of that until my mind was ready. Did I hear 'pregnant'? Back to business, Mr. James.

"Are you sure?" I asked.

"Yes."

"Is this what you want?"

"No."

I sneaked a look at her. She was trembling. She was fighting to control herself. "You see," she said through tight lips, determined for an instant. "I *do* get a grip on myself."

She dropped her head to her chest and cradled it in her hands. "Oh, God," she muttered. She lifted her head up again, took a deep breath, stared straight out through the windshield, still trembling. "I can do this," she said. "I *will* do this."

"How can I help?"

"There's nothing. Nothing really. It's my problem. I got myself into it, and now ..," sighed, "Just keep talking to me and listening to me. Be my friend."

"You know I am. I'll always be your friend."

"Damn!," she cried, then, "No, I didn't mean to say that. Not to you. Believe me." She jerked her head toward me. "But damn! Damn! One time, Jim. One time!" Her eyes were pleading. "I'm not even allowed one mistake? I can't make even one mistake?"

There she sat, her hands clasped in her lap. "I don't know what to do."

It suddenly struck me. In all our talking and all my plans, she had never known what to do. She just always did it. Never once had she said anything about her future. Not college, not a career or a job, not a family. Did the future even exist in her mind? I had a sudden chill. Let's get back to business, Mr. James.

"Have you seen a doctor?"

"No. I don't need to see a doctor."

"So –"

"There's .. there's … that's what it is." She sighed. "I missed last month. And then I just missed again. Trust me."

"Have you talked to your mother?"

"Of course. I had to. We talked like women. She reminded me that I was early myself. When *I* was born. So .. so far, so good with her."

"How about your dad? Does he know?"

"No one else does yet. I wanted to talk to you first, after my mother."

I had a sudden awful thought. "I have an awful thought. Want to hear it?"

"Why not? How much more awful can it be?"

"Like, you're not the only one. You're not alone in this. You know about Marsha? And that other girl, I'm not –"

"You mean Theresa? I thought no one knew!"

"So. What I'm saying is, You're not alone."

"Yes, I am."

I decided to let that thought hover in the air while I thought of something to say. Something that actually helped, if possible. Finally,

"No, you're not."

She nodded thoughtfully. "You know what really bothers me? It's not the baby. I mean, sure, it *is* the baby, but it isn't. It's that I don't know what to do now. And, it's like it doesn't matter. I thought I was making this big step. I was going to be a big girl, a grown-up, do the grown-up thing. Once and for all. Mistake. Now what do I do? I don't know."

Her voice became earnest. "Jim, thanks for letting me talk. Yes, I know I'm going to have a baby. And I know it's time for me to grow up and be a woman. I'm going to stand on my own two feet. I *will* do this. Why don't I believe a word of what I just said?"

Still thoughtful. "Jim, we've been friends since forever. Please be my friend now. I really appreciate when you support me and listen to me. I'll take it from there. It has to be my answers. Is that all right? But I need you. I don't know if I can do it without your support. I know I'm asking a lot of you."

So that was her story. She wanted my support but didn't want my advice; that was clear. She may have already guessed that, all the time we were talking, I was thinking that I should offer her marriage. Make an honest woman of her, as we used to say in those days. Whatever, she was telling me clearly that marriage was no part of her plans. As to the baby's father, he seemed totally out of the picture, he never existed. I wondered if Carolyn thought she was still a virgin.

Back at the house, after I'd driven her home, I sat for a long time in the living room, wondering if I should wake dad up. Eventually the bedroom door opened, and he came over to his chair by the heating stove.

Finally he said, "Problem?"

I shrugged – maybe.

"Carolyn?"

I nodded my head -- yes.

"You?"

I nodded my head – no.

I wanted to say, no, I'm not pregnant, but I knew if I did he would just huff and go back to bed. Instead, I told him everything that Carolyn and I had talked about, leaving nothing out.

"So that's where she thinks you come in? Nowhere?"

"Nowhere. I'm her friend. She was pretty emphatic about that. She's going to go ahead on her own."

"That sounds like our Carolyn. And where do *you* think you come in?"

I said I didn't know. "I'm her friend."

"You're thinking about marrying her," dad said. It wasn't a question, it was a statement.

"Doesn't matter what I think. She won't marry me."

"Give her time," dad said. "But think twice. Give yourself some time too. Think of your future. You want to kiss it all goodbye? And one more thing, Mr. James. You think you know her because you've always known her. Think again. That girl is not who she was. She's not little Carolyn any more. There's some real problem there. Don't get me wrong. She's a good kid. A great kid. You know how you've always liked her. I like her myself. But liking someone and marrying them are two different things. Time to think, Mr. James. Time to put that fine brain to work."

"I know, I know. But she needs me so much."

He nodded. There was more he could have said, but he didn't. He just shrugged and went back to bed.

A few minutes later, he came back out. "I'm just going to say one thing more, and I want you to listen."

"I'm listening."

"She's your best friend. You'll never have a friend like her, not even Mike and that Van Dorn character. But listen to me. Friendship and marriage are two completely different things."

"Yes, dad, I know." I'm sure I was smirking. Here comes the birds and the bees.

"You're right," said dad. "But that's not what I'm saying. Listen to me. Marriage is work."

"I know, dad. I've watched you and mom. I'm not blind."

He shook his head. He didn't think I was getting it. "I know you'll work. You always do. I'm not worried about that. Will she?"

"Doesn't matter. It isn't going to happen."

He stood up. "Marriage .. is .. work. Work. Think about it. Good night."

I turned off the table lamp and sat for a while longer in the darkness, but the Mr. James brain was done. We -- Mr. James and I -- did turn the same thoughts over and over again, until I fell asleep on the couch. I knew one thing: I was nowhere near as sure of myself as I might have made myself out to be.

(Years later, when he was in the clinic, dad told me he remembered that conversation clearly, how he wanted to say more, how he saw in complete clarity how it was going to end, and how there was no more point to saying anything further because he knew me, knew I was so determined. I was just going to have to find out for myself. As we talked then, he was having trouble breathing, but he went on. He had gotten pretty sick by then. He said, here is something even your mother never knew. He had gotten together with Carolyn's dad to hire a real detective. They wanted to find out who the guy was, the father. Then they, the dads, would put things right, whatever it took. But the shamus couldn't nail it down. Maybe the father lucked out, or maybe he got out. But he got away with it. Then dad had to call the nurse to turn his oxygen back on, and we would never get back to that conversation again.)

I needed to talk with someone besides dad, someone who wasn't already involved. My first thought was Father McIlhenny. He listened carefully and thoughtfully. He kept asking if I was sure that the child was not mine. I told him the whole story. He said pretty much what dad had said. He wondered what ways I could find to help support Carolyn without sacrificing myself.

My next stop was Mr. Craig, our English teacher. He was someone many of us talked to, and he knew Carolyn well. (We all learned from him. I particularly recall him saying once that *Life is simple; what's not is accepting that.* That's profound, I thought, so I stored it away until I could find an opportunity to apply it.)

In his office, I wasn't sure what I could say about her situation and what I couldn't, so I just said that she was my friend and that I was a little concerned about her. He gave me his 'professorial eyebrow of incredulity,' as we all used to call it, and asked me how well I really knew her. He added that she had often come to him and that he was concerned about her too, and had been for months.

His advice was that she might be having difficulties that were beyond my experience or abilities. She seemed to be, he said, "trapped in a mesh of her own devising." Is that the Bard? he wondered. He reached back in his mind. Maybe something like this? And he declaimed:

'Our wills and fates are so contrary
'That our plans are ever overthrown
'Our thoughts are ours, our ends run free of their own.'

He gave me a look that said; the Bard has spoken, what more need be said? Fortunately for me, he didn't stop there. He thought she might benefit from medical help, psychological help in particular. But he thought she would never accept it, "even if it were readily available, which it isn't, not around here." Not wanting to appear ignorant, I didn't ask what sort of help this help might be, but I memorized it phonetically -- 'si ko logical' – and made a mental note to look up the term as soon as I had the chance.

From the way he was talking, it seemed that he was unaware of her immediate situation. If he had been, somewhere in our time together he would have lifted an eyebrow again, or let the end of some sentence hang, but he didn't. Should I say something? Not my place. I didn't come to carry tales, and, if he didn't already know, how was it my place to tell him?

There was no one else I wanted to talk to, at least for now. I certainly did not want to bring the matter up with my friends. Of course Jack already knew, which meant that other people knew – he always said that secrets are like money, meant to be spent – but I didn't want to be the one to start the conversation.

A week after my discussion with Mr. Craig, one of my best friends (Mike Charney, if I ever mentioned him to you – yes, I did; he used to work on Carolyn's car) came to me. It seemed there were stories going around the school. What did I know? Coming from Mike, that was his way of saying that it's time to put some facts out there. But I didn't. I was fairly sure that Carolyn didn't care, but, once again, it was not my place to say something. Carolyn hadn't called since that night in the old Ford, and I knew her well enough to know that she would talk again when she was ready, and not before.

Jack did have a theory. "Might have been that kid from New York City," he said. It was plausible. This kid and his family had come up to the Valley every summer. This September, when the school year began, the mother and the kid stayed. She enrolled him at our school, and he made the consolidated Valley football team.

And then he was gone. Just like that. Word was that his parents had put him into a military academy back East.

"Might have been him."

Frankly I wanted to find the kid who did it. My plan was that I would then pound that kid, beat him up. What good that would do, I don't know, but I didn't think about that then. If it was the big city quarterback, he would do as well as anyone, if he ever came back.

But, when I talked with Mike about my so-called plan, he just said, Do the dates. So I did. I pointed out that he, the quarterback, was still here a month and a half ago. She said she'd missed two periods, so that put the beginning of the pregnancy sometime between the middle of September and the middle of October. He was still around until about the first week in October, which meant he was here when she got pregnant. Those dates work.

But Mike just repeated, do the dates. I said I've done the dates; now can I pound him if I can find him? I was getting very tough, especially as I realized there wasn't probably any way I'd ever see this kid again.

Mike just waited. What was he getting at? So? So, I wasn't done yet. And then it hit me. He may have gotten her pregnant, but he would not have known it. Whatever else he might have done, he hadn't run away from his responsibilities.

Mike kept waiting. Then it hit me again, finally. For someone who wanted to pound someone else, I was getting hit a lot myself. What hit me was that maybe what happened was as much her idea as his. Maybe more. Maybe she knew he was leaving. If she knew, it was her chance to show she could do it, to get that grip on herself, to be a woman at last; all those words she used. As I recalled her words, it all certainly tied together.

But then why all the tears? An act? No, I knew her tears, and those *were* her real tears. Was she at war with herself? 'Trapped in a web of her own devising' after all? Had she lost her nerve when the thought became an unexpected development? One point seemed likely, once I'd thought more about it: she'd only meant to lose her virginity, she had not planned on a baby at all. Also her words.

Mike said, "You, let it go. Don't do it." Jack said pretty much the same thing. They knew what I was thinking.

I thought of dad's words. 'Give yourself some time. Think of your future. Don't kiss it goodbye. Think, Mr. James. Time to put that fine brain to work.' But that was not where my brain's thoughts were going.

That Friday's game at Big Meadow was postponed. Their team was sick with a bug they had up their way; they couldn't put five healthy guys onto the court. So I used the night off to take a long drive -- up through the pass, play a few slots at the Buckhorn, head north past Buck Mountain by the lakes, a long stop at the now empty campground up there, and back home by midnight.

That drive gave me the time to think.

Go to college *with* her? Almost at once, I was not happy with that choice. There were just so many problems. Could I be a good student, and a good athlete, and a good husband, and a good father, all at the same time? Could I even be a good student, with the preparation I'd gotten? Too many kids from the Valley, especially guys, had come back with hefty debts and no diploma. They said the kids from down below were just too far ahead of them; they couldn't keep up.

And what about Carolyn? Here in Taylor she had as much support as she was ever going to have, and, even with all of that, I guessed she was barely managing. How would she ever handle being off in the Midwest somewhere with just herself and her infant and an overwhelmed husband?

How about college *without* her? The very thought was chilling almost immediately. I tried to think about concentrating on my studies and my game, and not thinking about her at all, and couldn't imagine myself succeeding.

By elimination, then, staying here seemed like the best choice. I wondered if I could keep my hand in by taking a course around here. The nearest live college courses were about forty miles away and over the mountains, with roads that were often impassible in winter. Maybe some sort of correspondence courses instead?

We, Mr. James and I, worked up a formula: Carolyn was now, college was not, but college could still be someday.

I made a plan. Suppose in tomorrow's game I could imagine that I was playing college ball on my own, far from home and Carolyn. And suppose I could play well anyway, stay on my game, clear my brain and concentrate. If I could do that, then maybe college was a possibility.

As I drove, I tried to play a whole quarter in my head. I wasn't successful. I couldn't stop thinking about her. How would I feel during the game? What game? All I could think about was Carolyn.

That was all there was to it. I knew it was disaster looming, but it was disaster no matter what, and I wanted to be inside looking out and not outside looking in. If anyone could bring her through, it was me. I didn't know if I could pull it off, but I had to try. And there was the baby. I trembled for that child when I thought of her as the mother, living with *her* mother, and with no one else to help. And since my college plan was a bird with a broken wing to begin with, I wanted to marry her now. As soon as possible.

Mr. James did manage to get a word in. Hold that thought, he said. See what happens in tomorrow's game. And then see how you still feel in a week. And that was the deal we made, Mr. James and me.

The next night I did everything in my power to imagine I'd left the Valley behind. In my mind it was the big time, not the Lumberjacks over in Pine Hill. Five thousand people were cheering in the stands, not the seventy-three that were actually there. We had four referees and a scoreboard with lights. No we didn't; we had one referee and a chalkboard with a kid erasing the score and writing a new one every time someone hit a basket. I didn't think I played well, but we won and I got some positive feedback on my performance. Inconclusive.

I decided to give it another week, to imagine my second option. The next week came along soon enough. A lengthy bus trip gave me time to think that we were already married, that she and the baby were in the stands, this was college, and we would be going back to our own little apartment after the game.

That night I stayed away from Mike and the other guys. I practiced my free throws at the other end of the court, did my stretches and sprints alone, kept my eyes down, did not speak. They seemed to understand; anyway, they all left me alone.

As soon as the game began, I checked the stands. Sure enough, I could picture Carolyn clearly. She even held up the baby. My heart pounded. I hoped the game would not go as it had with the Lumberjacks, that I would get at least some sort of answer.

I guess I did, but the game did not go according to my plan. The Garber Tigers were pathetic, it was not college, I sank seven shots and four free throws in the first half, Mike couldn't miss, Ash dominated the boards, and I was so focused on the game that I forgot to look up into the stands at all. By the time I remembered, it was the middle of the third quarter, all three of us were riding bench, and I couldn't picture baby and Carolyn at all. I wasn't sure what else I had proved, but I knew at least one thing: Basketball at college was in my future if I wanted it. Mr. James was saying, I told you so ..

.. but it didn't take. Heading back to Taylor on that long bus ride, somewhere deep down we both knew I wasn't going to any college any time soon if it was up to me, and we both hoped that Carolyn would have more sense than I did.

I was going to stop here, but I can't. There was one more thought on my mind in those days. I can't remember how it came up exactly, but it went something like this. Jesus says that we have a choice, to follow him or not. Specifically he says that the one who is not willing to follow Him at the cost of leaving his life behind -- mother and father, wife, brother, child -- is not worthy to follow Him. So I was stuck. I wasn't sure if or why Jesus wanted me to leave Carolyn to play basketball instead, but I wasn't going to leave her and that child behind. And yet I knew my heart was going to follow Him. It seemed impossible to me. Or are all things possible through Him? That thought, that conflict, has been a main driver of my life since then. Did I do the right thing? Another question I hope someday to ask Him.

All this time since our talk, Carolyn had not called, which was just as well for Mr. James if not for me. A couple of days after we had talked in the Ford, I did get a note from her. She apologized for 'snapping at me.' She hoped I would be pleased to know that she had talked to Theresa over lunch, was glad she had, and would keep talking with her. She had also tried talking to Marsha, but that didn't go as well. I wanted to send a reply, but was too torn about what to say, so I didn't. I think I still didn't know what to do, and I was so afraid of doing something wrong. Otherwise we had no contact.

That evening I did get a call, from another Gaertner. Her father. Her father! What did he want? Whatever else he wanted, he wanted to see me. At ten o'clock sharp tomorrow. In his old office, at the market. I told him I would get back to him just as soon as I could, but I had to go, I was right in the middle of something that couldn't wait, and basically hung up on him. Then I called dad, who was working late, and he told me to come right up.

The sawmill where dad worked is gone now – all the mills that were anywhere around here are gone. Where dad worked is now the town park and the court and the fields. The only traces left of the mill itself are the historical plaque under the flagpole and the employee's parking lot, which is now the parking lot for the park, which was where dad was waiting for me.

We walked over to his office, where it was warmer and more comfortable. I remember following him and taking a deep breath, which calmed me – I always loved the damp smell of sawdust.

In the office the other clerk left when we came in. Dad pushed his ledger aside, his heavy, leather-bound ledger with its own wonderful smell.

"Monthend stuff." He shook his head. "Taxes, W-2's, statements, audit prep. Not like the old days."

"Well, you got a job out of it."

"True. I guess I really don't have a beef. Before I got your call, I was going to tell you when I got home that I saw Carolyn's dad in town. Wondered then if he was looking for you."

"Did you talk to him?"

"Didn't. He was on his side of the street, going out, and I was on my side, going in. Just as well. Probably better to mind my own business. What did he say that he wanted?"

"He didn't. I didn't give him the chance, but I think I can guess. Whatever it is, exactly, he's going to come down on me like a ton of bricks. He already did. And all I am to him is her old friend."

Dad sat back. "Might be an opportunity here. Let's think about it together, Mister. You've been thinking. What do *you* want from this?"

Me, meditative: "Too-too, too-too, too-ra-loo. I know you're right, but I'm not going to leave her. Maybe she'll have more sense than I do."

"Have you worked anything out with her?"

"No. I'm waiting for her to come to me."

"Good. I guess. So what about him? What are you going to say?"

"That's why I'm here. What do you think? What should I say? Should I even go? What can I say if I do?"

Dad: "Do you have to say anything? You could just listen. Remember, he may have the chips, but you have the cards. You know his cards and he doesn't know yours, he only thinks he does. So why show them for nothing? See what he's offering first. And remember everything, because you're probably going to have to go to him some day."

He went on. "Another thing. Once he makes up his mind, nothing stops him. He's a good man, but he's a horse's ass, a bull in a china shop, isn't he?" He waited for a response, didn't get one. "Maybe shouldn't have said that, I guess. One of our leading citizens. But, Mr. James, let's keep thinking about the opportunity. Play the cards right. Let's think on this – suppose you *don't* see him?"

"If I don't see him, he's angry. He's used to getting his way. Like you say, he's a bull. He won't take no for an answer."

"So, you *do* see him. Then what happens?"

"If I say nothing?"

"See what cards he puts on the table. He's going to think he knows it all. As long as you have to see him anyway, what have you got to lose?"

"*If* I can say nothing."

"Good work, Mr. James. What else does Mr. James think?"

"Nothing much. Just stay loose, pick my spots, let it come to me."

"Like basketball?"

"Like basketball."

"Need me around?"

"You're busy, and I think I have this. Let me see if I can handle it this time. But be ready."

"Can do. I'm trying to remember – how well do you get along with her mom?'

"Got along pretty well with her, before." Before they left, I meant. "Now, with the drinking .. You know about the drinking? But. I can tell you what she's going to say. She's going to say, I always knew it would be you for her."

"She's had a hard life. And you, you have your work cut out for you. Well! Anything else?"

"Can't think of it. Will you be home in an hour?"

"Another hour. Care for a quick snort before you go? A little relaxer?"

"A what?"

He pulled two shot glasses and a bottle from behind the files in the lower left drawer of his desk. He filled the glasses, handed me one across the desk, and sat back, holding his glass up.

I said, "Here's to fathers."

"And grandfathers?" We clicked glasses. He looked deeply into the dark glass. "Hello, grandfather," he said to his reflection.

And I thought to myself, so that's it then. Just two more steps.

"Come on in and sit down. Glad you're here. You can call me Jack. Listen, I know some people around here don't think I've been the father I should have been to my daughter, but I want you to know that there's nothing I wouldn't do for her. Do you understand?"

"Yes, sir."

"Call me Jack. Do you understand?"

I didn't answer

"Do .. you .. understand?"

"I'll try, sir. It's a bit difficult for me." I'm sure he thought I was awed by his great and mighty adulthood, to the point where I could hardly deal with his self-proclaimed equal footing. How could I explain that it wasn't that at all, that I already had one Jack and wasn't sure how to fit another one in? I needed a few minutes to think that one through. Maybe the 'Jack' would come in time. Or, try calling him Big Jack in my mind? In the meantime, don't push me. "Perhaps it might be better if my dad were here?"

"Nonsense, we can work this out just between us two, don't you think? I think we can. Now, listen, I want you to know that everything is already settled. So that's that. We're giving you everything we can to get you off to a good start. After that, you realize, it's up to you. People around here think I have a lot of money. I don't." I thought I saw his face quiver momentarily. "But when my little girl is involved, you call me. Do you understand? You call me. You have my word on that." He gave me his business card. Numbers were written on it in pencil. "Those are my private numbers. Now here's what I want from you. But I don't have to go into that, do I? I've known you since you were .. a little kid, and I've never known you to do anything but the right thing. There's no one I'd rather see with my daughter than you. I can count on you to do right by her. Am I correct?"

"Uh, Mr. Gaertner .. "

"Now, women are not bad people once you get to know them. You just have to make some allowances. Take my situation.

Now it's true that my wife and I are not together at the moment. That's what we've had to do to keep our love alive. So you see what I mean. We make the adjustments we need to make ..." He spent the next half hour or so telling me about marriage and women and how to handle them, which from the man's side was mostly about money. He told me how to get ahead in business, which was to do what you have to do without hesitation or remorse, and then how to raise children, which was to get out of the way and let the women handle it all, no man will ever understand and can only make things worse if he tries.

I tried again to stop him -- "Yes, but first there's something .. " – without success. A balancing act. I didn't really want to stop him yet, just to be able to say that I had tried until I'd heard him out.

"… just as soon as I've shown you around, introduce you to a few people here. We're almost done. But first there's something I want you to see."

He opened a drawer and slapped a weapon down on the desk blotter. An automatic. "In case my words aren't enough to tell you how much my daughter means to me ..."

To be honest, my instantaneous reaction was fear. I *was* afraid. You slap a weapon down like that, it can go off. My second reaction was incredulity. It was clear already that he didn't know any more than I did about handling weapons, if that was possible.

I fought to hide my reaction but did not completely succeed.

"Are you laughing? Is there something here you find funny?"

"No, sir, I have nothing but respect for weapons." And that was when I had the wild idea. I still don't know what got into me. The Devil? Dad?

Mr. Gaertner was sitting there stone-faced, four feet away from me, rigid, glaring, wordless.

"May I take a look at it?" Expecting no reply, I gently picked the weapon off his desk and turned it over and around in my hands, using up time while I formed my thoughts. Go for it.

"An Ivers Johnson, isn't it? Made in Springfield? Takes a special bullet? I didn't know you could get bullets for one of these things any more. Kind of dirty, isn't it? Want me to take it and try cleaning it up for you?"

Total bluff. I was making all this up as I went along. Ivers Johnson didn't even make automatics.

But he fell for it. Busted!

"No, I don't think that will be necessary." He held out his hand, took the weapon back. "And now that we understand each other, I guess .. there's, well, no need for this." He returned it to the desk drawer and leaned forward, his elbows on the blotter and his head in his hands. Respect? "But now there's something I don't understand. My wife said my daughter told her that you're not the father? She's insisting you're not."

I'd seen his cards, and he knew it. Now he wanted to see mine. Why not? I'd played this long enough. "No, sir. And Carolyn and I have made no plans together. I'm sorry that I did not express myself more emphatically about that right up front."

"No matter. It'll all work itself out. Listen, I was doing what I had to do. When you're a father, you'll understand." He sat back. "But you're *not* the father?" he mused. "So why are you doing this?"

"Doing what? Sir, we've made no plans. There are no plans between your daughter and myself."

"Everyone I've talked to says that you and my daughter are getting married. Everyone. My wife, the people here in the store who know you, the people down at city hall. Everyone. And you're saying it's not so?"

"Did Carolyn say it?"

"Well, not exactly. But …"

"Sir, I have to say, if it's not according to Carolyn, then it's not happening, and hers is the vote that counts. And now, sir, if you'll excuse me, I think someone needs to bring her into the discussion. Thank you for talking to me, and I appreciate your advice and your concerns. She's as good a friend as I have, and I'm very concerned about her too." Whatever else we said, I did NOT want him to ask me about *my* vote, about what I wanted.

"Understood. Sometimes .. but listen, Jim, we've had our little talk and I'm glad we did. I think we understand each other now just fine. But everything I said before still stands. That child is going to need someone strong to depend on, and I can't be here. So think about it. And listen, if you ever do find out who the father is, just make sure you keep him away from me. Because, if I ever meet up with him," pointing to his desk drawer with the pistol inside, "This time there'll be no fooling around."

Driving to school was when the rest of it came to me. As dad said one time, If you ever do get an interest in playing cards, and it's not a bad thing if you do, remember this: The fellow who lives by the bluff is the fellow who will fall for a bluff. So it wasn't the devil after all, just my father's advice coming back to me.

And I thought about that weapon on the desk, and how useless it was in that situation. That's the first time I remember thinking about what kinds of questions could be answered with weapons, and how often those answers weren't answers at all, just a step toward worse questions. Dad was a veteran – Korea – and he once said, if you want peace, put a general in charge. A real general, someone who's seen war: Washington, Grant, Eisenhower. No one who's really seen war ever wants one.

In school that afternoon I was feeling pretty good about life in general and myself in particular.

At one point I did run into Carolyn in the halls and we talked briefly. She did not seem to know about my discussion with her father.

Not so the next day. That morning when I got to school, I couldn't park. A car, familiar, was already in my regular spot, under the trees by the highway. Carolyn got out of the car – her mother's, actually – and into mine. "Get me out of here. Please. Just forget about your classes."

I drove out of the school lot and headed out toward Willow Camp. When the school was well behind us, she sighed. "My mother and my father had such a fight last night. She was furious. She's even mad at you. Why did you even talk to him?"

'Carolyn, maybe it was a bad idea, but I didn't see any way not to, and neither did my dad. It was your dad that called me, not the other way around, and you know how your father is when he wants something. I don't know what you might have been told, but I want you to know that I was as clear as I could be that we have no plans together, and I didn't say anything about you or what I think your plans are because it's none of my business."

"Okay, okay, I should have known. I feel so helpless."

"I can imagine. He never even talked to you first, did he?"

"That was one of the things my mother brought up. In the discussion."

"I can imagine. For whatever it's worth, he seems to think that we've got a future all planned out. Do you mind if I ask, how well does this man who is your father actually know you?"

"A fine question, my fine friend. That was something she said when she tore into him. Actually, I felt bad for him. I've haven't seen her like that since before he left. He couldn't get a word out. Finally he just got up and went away. I don't know where he is now. I think he's gone."

"And you were there? That must have been tough."

"She wanted me there. You know what she said to him? She said, 'Who invited Jim to the party? And who invited you? Carolyn is taking care of this, and she doesn't need your help or anybody else's. But you don't get it. To you she's just a side of beef! Hanging in the locker! Check the price on it and let's haggle! You didn't even talk to her!' Wow. She was tough. My mother is a good person, but she can be maybe sometimes a little bit too horribly and completely and totally relentless occasionally from time to time." A bitter smile.

"I think she loves you very much. He does too."

I'd parked under the willows where no one could see the car from the road. In the middle of the day no one else was around. "Is this a good place?"

"This is fine." She stared at the clock on the dashboard. "Jim, what am I going to do? And do please let me know when you get tired of hearing that question."

"I believe you're going to have this baby. You're going to grow up and be a woman. You're going to take care of this and you don't need anyone's help."

"Very true, I suppose. Pretty ambitious for a side of beef, don't you think? And I deserve that. What am I thinking?"

"It's not that bad. … You do have some … Hey, there's your dad, he will give you at least as much help as you can possibly need from him and maybe even more ..."

I was remembering the last time I offered advice to her, and was trying to stop myself. Also, somewhere in the back of my mind, some other words were starting to ready themselves, and I wanted to let myself hear them.

She cut me off. "… I'm sorry. You're just trying to help. And I appreciate it. My life is such a mess. Now, Jim, " -- she was calming down, breathing more easily. "Help me on this. I've got a choice. I can be a side of beef here. Or I can leave everything and everyone I've ever known and start all over in a strange place with no skills, no connections, and an infant I'm raising by myself." After a minute, she added, "So I don't know what to do. Tell me about you. Have you decided about your choices yet? You were talking about college. And basketball."

"Yes, but you're not going to like my answer."

"That's all right, I don't like my answer either. I do know what you're thinking, you know. I know you by now. So let's talk about you for a change. Let's face it, I know you'll be there for me, but I can manage basically. My father will always help. I can go to school and learn bookkeeping. Maybe working with kids. Waitressing, even. So, call me a side of beef. There is something to be said for being a side of beef. At least you're still part of the community."

"And being consumed locally."

"Yeah, I know," she said wearily.

That's when I opened my mouth. "You asked a question. May I tell you my answer, what I'm thinking? You may not like it, but it will work for me. And that is, Going, staying, it really doesn't matter to me." Here we go, Mr. James; hope you've got this. "What does matter is, wherever I go, whatever I do, it'll be where you are. And I'll do it with you if you'll let me. That's my rock. You can leave me, whatever, and I'll understand, but there's no way on this earth I'm leaving you. And that's that."

She listened. She sighed. "I think I knew you would say something like that. And I appreciate it. But suppose that doesn't work for me?'

"Then *you* leave. Or *you* push me away. *You* never speak to me again. You dangle me halfway out in space. You stay, and you marry someone else. You marry someone else and go away. You don't know what to do. You do one thing one day and another tomorrow. All the same to me. You can leave me, but I will never leave you as long as I have any choice in the matter. And that's that."

In her quiet voice, she said, "Let's get out of the car."

We walked over toward the pond.

The air was still, so the sun took some of the chill out of the air. Not a ripple broke the water anywhere. No birds: no swan, no duck. Odd. Crisp air.

A boat was pulled up on the rocky shore. I asked her if she wanted to go out onto the water and she said she didn't. She wanted to walk around the pond. "I'm thinking about what you said. I don't like it. It's stupid. You can have a life. Why would you want to do this?"

"You are part of my life. Part of me. I'm less without you. Simple as that."

"And suppose you're not part of *my* life. Suppose I don't even have a life. What then?"

What was she saying? I felt that chill, and it wasn't just the air. But I was determined not to start giving her advice. "Like I said. Don't know. Keep breathing, survive, find someone or something. Not what I want, but I'll live."

"By the way, you must know I would never dangle you in space."

"Just being dramatic. Thinking of the worst that could happen."

She squinted. We were out from under the trees. "Let's walk over to that cinder cone."

"Want to climb it?"

"I might. Have you ever climbed it? Out here with your friends? Drinking beer?"

I ignored the crack about beer. "Yeah, I've climbed it. You get lots of grit in your shoes. Not much view. If I want a view, I go over to the lookout at the pass."

"Let's go back to the car then. This side of beef is getting chilled." Then she said, "I'm the same as you. I don't know what my life would be without you in it."

Keep going, I thought. This is as good a time as any. She'll say No? Let's just get it out there and see what happens. Let's just do it. Don't look at her.

"I have a thought, Carolyn. Let's just do it. Let's drive right over to the chapel at StateLine and do it. Right now. Just do it and get it behind us."

"What?"

"We *are* going to get married, Carolyn. Is there a shred of doubt in your mind? And -- "

"*-- Jim! --*"

" – no one needs to know. We don't have to say a word to anyone. Not your folks. Not mine. We're both eighteen. All we need is that piece of paper. But you'll know in writing that someone will always be there beside you if you want them. If things don't work out, tear it up and dump me. I'll never say a word. I'll make it as easy for you as I can. You're crying .. ?"

"No, I am not crying." Yes, you are. *"I can't do that. I can't run away."*

"Maybe I shouldn't have ..."

"*.. No, no, that's not it. I want a wedding. A real wedding.* I've always wanted a wedding."

"Think on it. A week and then let's talk again?"

"Give me a minute." She caught her breath.

I wanted to shut myself up, but I couldn't. "There's nothing to stop us. We can be married now, just us, no one else, and then have a wedding then, a real wedding. I'm sure your dad will put out the spread of a lifetime for his daughter."

"Oh, my father! That's funny! I meant to ask, did my father really pull a gun on you?"

"Not exactly. And I'm so sorry I, well, I sort of laughed at him. I made fun of his weapon. I hope he didn't take it the wrong way."

"You what?! You did? That's wonderful! Let me tell you, I know my dad and, whatever happened, he did *not* take it the wrong way. He's so impressed with you, Jim. Whatever you did, you won him over completely. That's what he said. He said, 'That Jim of yours. He may look like a boy, but there's more than enough man to him. Don't you ever lose him.' But Jim," turning serious again, "There's not that much to *me*. As a side of beef, I mean. Will I ever be enough woman for you? Just as I am? Because, if we do this, you are never never ever getting rid of me," and I think she added, "As long as I live."

But she still wasn't ready. It wasn't until a week later to the day that we drove over to StateLine. We went alone. And that was that.

Saturday, December 13

No meteor shower last night: too cloudy, so did my Friday routine. Buckhorn very peaceful, thankfully. Fellow there who I hadn't seen before who had a theory about the future of the genders. He believes that in two or three hundred years there will be women specially bred to have children, and there'll be all this genetic engineering so that the rest of the women won't have children at all, won't even have periods or a uterus. The ones who can't have children of their own can get children to raise, but only if they apply and are accepted, like going to college today. That way, there'll be no abortions, and no kid will be raised in poverty, or unwanted, or with crazy parents. 'It'll all be like the ants, see? Ever see how they all work together?'

What about men?, I asked. He said, Won't be any. There'll be enough sperm banked for a thousand years, and by that time they'll be able to make all the sperm they need. No call for men at all. Don't hardly need men now, really.

I guessed that he had more on his mind that he wanted to talk about, but I couldn't get him to open up beyond his one idea, so I let him talk himself out. Eventually he noticed a lady at the bar who might still have some use for a man, so he started off, stopped, apologized - sorry, father, but I have to do this. I understand, I said, but think about what we were just talking about. Come back when you're ready. I'll be here just about every week.

Should I have said more? Never feel right as to how to handle this, but still working on 'judge not.' Thought about it all the way home; too much to go into here. Keep thinking.

[Later] Better sky for meteors tonight, but only a few streaks. Back when I was a kid, it was a real shower, sometimes two and three streaks at a time. Doesn't make sense that a few earth years should make any difference to those heavenly bodies. So was the meteor shower really better when I was a kid? How could a meteor shower have changed in my lifetime? Is it my memory? My eyesight? Some change in the atmosphere?

With the cold in the garden at that hour, and winter coming, the warmth of the tropics is alluring. I was warmed just thinking about it. I could see the sparkling, clear, intensely blue waters, dotted with sails or the fishermen's canoes. (Were there fishermen there? I couldn't remember. Definitely divers. Does it matter?)

What would I be doing there if I went?

Maybe I shouldn't be thinking of a trip like this as a place to go to do something. Maybe I should go to be done unto.

Maybe I should go there to learn. Go around, talk to the ministers, see what everyone needs and how they go about meeting their needs: food, clothing, housing, social services, childcare, jobs. Essentially something like a larger version of my beer ministry here.

Heard from Hal, late. Woke me up. Familiar voice on the phone. I repeated what I had asked in my letter about Carolyn – could I send him more? His answer: "Hey, dumbbutt, thanks for sharing. You're breaking my heart. Now what do I have to do? Come out there and kick your heinie?"

"So, what are you saying? Do you want to read more?"

"Padre, here's what you can do. Go fornicate yourself," he said, and hung up. I took that as a 'Yes.'

Sunday, December 14

Tough night last night. Headed over to the pass to see any more meteor shower from there, but didn't. The pass was closed. There'd been a big accident, but they waved me through when they saw it was me. Semi got shoved over by the wind up there into a sports car, hit it almost head on. Truck driver very shaken and upset but otherwise all right, as far as I could tell -- go find him and talk to him again tomorrow if I can. Not so for the couple in the sports car, if you could still even see a car in that tangled mess. One of the EMTs said that she might still be alive, so I blessed her and talked to her while they cut the car open to get her out. Then came back here to clean up and decided I'd seen enough for one night. Never have gotten used to crushed bodies and blood smeared and dripping everywhere, don't expect I ever will.

This morning called the hospital early. The couple was DOA, of course. The driver of the truck had already been checked out by his son. Taking him back to Omaha, the desk person thought she heard them say. The driver was still shaking and red-faced even though they'd sedated him. Said he didn't know if he could ever go back to driving again.

Saw their pictures on the morning newscast, the couple in the sports car, realized I knew them from the Casino. Probably headed there last night.

[Later] Couldn't sleep, so sat up and worked on the Carolyn. Helped.

Monday, December 15

Servant heart --

- Stop. Breathe. In. Out.
- Go see dad and Carolyn (and clean up around some other graves)
- Then to the Methodists? See Dan.
- See Missus B.
- Home baptism Wednesday
- Hospital *Wednesday* <u>THIS WEEK ONLY!</u>
- Also Wednesday: Carl Beltramba.
- Take Little Mike out to lunch
- Homily. *What?*
- Send Hal the 'Old Fords.' I mean, he asked for it.

Called the foreman at the mall job and told him I wouldn't be making it in today, also called one of my summer people where I'd arrranged to come in for an hour after work; put off both jobs until tomorrow. I didn't mention the accident. The summer people don't want to know that we have our troubles up here just like they do down there. Cleaned up the last of the blood in the bathroom, still some stains in the car even though I scrubbed. Couldn't shoot a three to save myself, so went out to Willow Camp to see about the swans. That didn't help. Looks like nothing's helping at the moment.

[Later] Stayed up very late and worked:

Dear Hal,

So here's the rest of my story. Sorry about going on with this for so long, but when one lets it out, one has to let it all out.

By the way, as far as I'm concerned, all of this whole vast epic can be public, in case anyone asks. The only person I care about who might have had a problem with anything here would have been Erin (my daughter), but she knows. She's fine with it, makes no difference to her at all, I am and always have been her father, and that's that. She and her mother are so much alike, she's a little more serious but not much.

Thanks for letting me go on this, and thanks for your (fornicating!) support. In case you're wondering, if I had the opportunity to do it all over again with her, Carolyn, I would, without hesitation. He doesn't promise happy endings in this life, only a life that is full and abundant, and I feel it flowing into me more strongly every day. Where would I be if I had not had this experience? At least, that's the approved answer I tell myself. Starting to believe it.

Where are you now, with your son and your family, your business? Phone calls (especially yours!) are not enough. Let's get together, but call first, because I might be headed out of town.

You'll see where I'm talking about the clinic in the enclosed. I'd love to show it to you. Do you know about it? Have you ever seen it? There's been a few changes since she was there. (I have to add, one of those changes would be the new hospice ward: the Carolyn Gaertner Lawrence Pavilion. The Big Jack really did do everything money could do.) Maybe we could go over together. Actually, I think I might really appreciate you being there with me. And maybe you still do owe me one?

Your friend,
Jim

.. Still Haunt Me

So, we were married. Nothing changed, and everything did. My thinking – our thinking – changed utterly. Now it wasn't me; it was us. We had something unshakeable that only we shared. That was our secret, and ours alone. We went on as before, of course – she at her mother's, me at my parents'. It seemed to me that we were actually a little more distant in public. Yet the looks we exchanged were incandescent. Every time I saw her, she was glowing. I felt like I was glowing myself. I felt like we were on a stage, crowded with people, but the spotlights were on us and us alone.

What didn't change was everything else. I couldn't understand how no one saw how different we were. Our secret couldn't possibly last a week.

Inside, I must have craved to be the center of attention. I wanted a movie moment, one where I would enter the scene from one side and Carolyn from the other, and all our friends and neighbors would part as we walked slowly through the crowd to center stage, holding hands and singing a duet while they would step back to form into a chorus, and the voices and the violins would soar behind us.

Or we would suddenly find ourselves in a wonderfully sparkling unreal kitchen, washing dishes and singing, always singing, with adorable cartoon bluebirds fluttering about and chirping merrily, and our impossibly photogenic toddler radiant in the background.

But no one around us noticed anything at all.

Mike was having some sort of spat with his current girlfriend. She wasn't spending time at lunch with us anymore out in the schoolyard. She was with a circle of the girls, five feet away, with her back to us and Mike's back to her.

Jack was excited about a scheme whereby he would set up a clearing house to get handyman jobs and then match the jobs with willing kids that he'd signed up. While he took a cut, of course. "See, the kumquats do all the work, ol' Jack doesn't lift a finger, and the money rolls in, what do you think? No problem, eh?"

Dad was looking at houses, and had me come along. If you do go away to college, he said, this house will be a rental, and we have a story that will work for anyone who asks. If you don't go away, having you help to fix it up would teach you carpentry skills for the future. Who knows, he said without a change of expression, straight-faced, maybe one of these days you might have a family, and you'll want a house. If you do go to college, you might still want a house here down the line, if you come back.

He had been thinking about a particular house, an abandoned place on Polk Street, only a couple of blocks away from us. Dad and I and the real estate agent went to take a look at it. On the way, the agent couldn't tell us much about the house, but assured us the owner was eager to sell. At the house, waiting, was a contractor that dad knew.

From the street the house was basically awful. No one had lived there for several years. The yard was overgrown. Peeling plywood covered the windows. Inside was a mess: the walls were torn up and scrawled on, the floor was covered with trash, the whole place smelled, and there clearly had been a family of mice under the kitchen sink.

Downstairs, the basement was dry. Dad and the contractor shined their flashlights, poked at the floor joists and the foundation masonry with screwdrivers, carefully inspected the wiring and the plumbing connections. Visually the systems looked functional, but the heating and plumbing would definitely need to be tested before any offer was made.

Dad and the contractor went up to the attic without us. I'm not sure why, probably to talk. When they came down, he shrugged, said I could go up if I wanted to.

Outside – it was almost too smelly to stay inside – dad wrote up a preliminary punch-list while he, the realtor, and the contractor talked. Somehow get an exterminator immediately, even before the offer if they'll pay. Have the power and water turned on, do a thorough check on the systems. Work up estimates for new windows downstairs, a new bathroom, new wallboard throughout, 'shoulder joists' in the attic. Live with the kitchen for now and wait on the porch and the upstairs until there was more time and money.

"Well, Mr. James, what do *you* think?"

What did I think? I didn't want to think about that house at all. It was a pile of junk, it'd never be anything else. But what did I know? Say something. "I'm concerned about that smell."

The smell is nothing, they assured me. It means the house is not far from air tight. Sure, it's old and needs a lot of work, but it's basically sound; the systems are antiquated but probably functional; the appliances should work a while longer; and you've got town water and sewer, no problem there. When you've got a roof and a basement, you've got a house. Appearance is nothing; it's just a little money and a lot of sweat. As to the smell, it's rotted food and animal smell and the poor ventilation from the years of being closed up. Once the exterminator is done and the place is cleaned up, leave the windows open for a week, and you'll be breathing easy. It's not a musty smell; water damage isn't a problem.

I wanted to say something affirmative but noncommittal, so I observed that it was the worst house in the neighborhood, which is supposed to be good. They were already talking; I don't think they heard me.

After dad thanked his contractor friend, we told the realtor we'd get back to her and she left for her office. Then the two of us took the long way home. You don't like it, he said, but we might have a deal here. We'll plan the work and get the materials and the permits together while you concentrate on school. Then you'll bust your keister. Once spring comes, you'll start right away on the yard, and we'll bring you in on the jobs inside as they are being done, teach you all we can. If you're staying, you'll need to make a living, and a good carpenter always eats.

In his mind, I thought, we'd already bought the house.

Here's my idea, he said. Let's not wait for the systems review and the exterminator. Let's just try a really lowball offer, say that we'll take the property totally 'as is.' Try $500 cash, take it or leave it. Call back in a couple months if they don't bite.

We must have gone over all our plans for at least an hour when we stopped for lunch at StateLine. I still wasn't happy. I brought up everything I could think of, brought up the sewer and water lines. Suppose those had to be redone? There has to be a reason why they walked away, whoever they are. Looking back, I realize I probably wasn't ready.

But think about the possibilities, he said. And look at the worst case. The worst case is, they accept, and it doesn't work out, like you say. We kiss our $500 goodbye, and we find a way to walk away too. Life is short, there's always risk, there's risk on both sides.

By the time we got home, I had agreed, but I still couldn't imagine that house being livable. I quietly hoped the owners would not accept.

They did; they accepted the offer. Just like that. I was a homeowner.

Around that time the basketball scholarship the coach had talked about came through. It was not quite as good as he had described – partial tuition, and only for as long as I was on the team, no part-time guaranteed job, and only a small stipend for housing. Coach said it was still a good offer, but they were concerned that I was too thin. They wanted someone more physical. Also, I had not yet shown myself against high-level competition. He advised waiting. We were all but certain to make it to the North State Regionals, a real showcase for me and for the team.

Carolyn and I talked about the offer but couldn't concentrate on it. We had too much else on our minds. Being married. The wedding someday. We wanted to enjoy our secret for as long as we could, the almost unreal thought that we were actually already married. We talked about the house and all that went with the house, and was the house even going to be a place where we could live? (She was aghast when I first showed it to her.) We talked about everything, on the phone for hours every night, face-to-face at least once a week: at Willow Camp, behind the garage, over lunch, at the truck stop off the Interstate.

One night at Willow Camp we were making out – making out! – when she pulled away. With lowered voice and head, she said, "There's something you need to know before we go all the way with this – the wedding, I mean." I could hardly hear her. "I don't know if I'll be able to give you a family." She was having trouble controlling herself. She cried: "Jim, it was awful. It was the worst experience of my life. We were both idiots. Wrestling around in his stupid car. Ick and goo and everything else everywhere."

"Was it .."

"No." She calmed herself down. "It was all my idea. The girls in the locker room said he was smooth. I just wanted to do it and get it over with. He said we would be safe. What a mistake. He didn't know any more than I did. Jim! Dirty, messy, wet, slimy, everything was slipping around, it fell off and we couldn't find it, he couldn't, he couldn't .. I couldn't .. I tore my dress on the door handle. Did I ever tell you how I cut myself? I wasn't even sure we'd actually done it. I guess we did." Bitter laugh.

A car went by in the distance, lighting the treetops momentarily in its headlights.

The engine was running in our car. It was cold. It's cold at night out here, even before the snow. I touched her hand -- also cold.

'I'll say it once more. It was all my idea. I have no one to blame but myself." She threw herself on me. "I don't know if I'll ever be able to give you a family," she cried.

I was nervous. More of my future was disappearing. But I spoke up bravely, with all the courage I could gather. "Carolyn, it's all right. That's not a problem. You know that's not what we're about. You know I'll never hurt you. I'll wait forever if that's what it takes." I knew my lines.

"Jim, are you listening? It might *be* forever. Can you stand that?"

"For you?"

Thoughtful. "Like you said, you don't have to do this. We can tear up the license, not have the wedding, you'll still be in my life, and you'll *have* a life. I'm saying, you don't have to do this. I'll understand. We'll still be best friends forever." She sounded like my dad.

Think, Mr. James. This is important. Sure, some guy will come along, and they'll marry, but I'll always be her best friend? How long will that guy last? Or, we'll tear it up, and then she won't ever marry, and neither will I. Say something. What'll I say? Say a line. Get it right.

"Is that what you want?" My expression and diction were superb. One take on this one.

"Oh, Jim, I want to be the best wife to you that you could ever have!"

All that while we had been having very good times at Willow Camp. Limits were established. Our unspoken rule was, no buttons unbuttoned, no zippers unzipped, no special way of dressing, except that she stopped wearing dresses and started wearing jeans. And it was good.

She was so relaxed then, more so than I'd ever seen her. Noise was made. Clothing was ruffled. The car was rocked. We even tried sharing a cigarette when it was time to catch our breath, like they did in the movies, but both of us got queasy, and we did not repeat that experiment.

Except for the wedding we did not talk about the future at all, and we barely talked about that. We did not even think about the other person in the car, the tiny miracle that would be Erin. We knew we had a wedding somewhere in the future, but we wanted the time now to ourselves, to enjoy our secret together for as long as we could. We knew we were running out of time.

Those good times lasted a month. Then the cramps started. Although she didn't show, she started having trouble keeping food down. The doctor put her on a special diet, but she didn't care for the food. She really wasn't interested in food at all, but she tried to eat for the baby.

Just before Christmas we decided to tell mom (dad knew) and her parents about our plans, and I told the coach. There wasn't much time if we didn't want to be seen carrying a baby down the aisle. It turned out that the parents had already started the planning. They'd already scouted the place, the minister, the music, the photographer, the decorator, and the food, and even had set a tentative date. All they had needed was us.

And what a wedding we had. It was truly a 'grand affair,' as my grandmother dubbed it, and what a surprise it was to see her again, all the way from the old country. The Big Jack did definitely do it right, all of it. We had bubbling fountains in every corner and a naked Venus de Milo in ice as the middle of the floor, except this time it had arms, because a broken statue was just not acceptable for a centerpiece, 'no matter what those fairy caterers said.' Two bands took turns, um-pah-pah for the old people and Rocking Johnny for us. The food was excellent and never stopped coming. And we had grandma. I can still see her on the dance floor, skirt high, feet flying, as she showed us how they celebrated back when her hair was red and all the world was green.

At the altar, Carolyn was brave. She had taken her medicines and was pale. Mike couldn't find the ring. Dad was ready to save the day by offering his, but then Jack, my Jack, remembered he had it all along. They had done a great job with her dress; she didn't show. Probably everyone knew, but they certainly didn't say anything.

We barely had any time to ourselves after the vows. Every so often, as we made our separate ways around the floor, our eyes would meet. She would smile. She seemed weak but happy.

I met so many people, and they all told me not to worry about remembering names as they gave me their envelopes or slipped by to leave them on the table by the thrones where Carolyn and I were supposed to be sitting but hardly ever were.

At one point coach pulled all the other guys together and we did the team cheer – Vikings fight! Vikings win! Vikings RULE! -- to the great appreciation of the local guests, sports fans all, and the bafflement of everyone else.

Carolyn was surrounded by the girls from the school in their crinoline dresses. They were laughing and shrieking together, and for once she was a part of it.

Dad introduced me to all the people who would be working on the house. I finally got to meet the electrician. The plumber pulled me aside for a moment, to ask about the bathroom sink fixtures: Did we want modern or traditional? (I said that we'd have to get back to him on that.)

There was toast after toast. Jack, my Jack, bless him, had made sure with our waiter that our champagne glasses were filled with ginger ale.

Carolyn had said that she was going to tell her mother, on a vow of secrecy, after the cake was cut, that we were already married. A few minutes later her mother came bustling over to me. "There's my husband for you. His name is Jack, he's spending all his jack, and he doesn't know jack." She couldn't stop laughing.

At some point Mike came over and told me that his girlfriend told him some of the girls were getting tipsy in the lady's room, and did I want him to do something about it? At the time I didn't realize he was trying to tell me that Carolyn probably was one of them.

Eventually dad reminded me that no one would want to leave until we did, so I led Carolyn out while everyone applauded. Outside there was a surprise: a brand-new Ford decorated with a trail of tin cans and with 'Just Married' scrawled in whitewash on the doors and back window. People were throwing flowers and rice. Mike had said he was going to lob a basketball, but of course the whole team had left early for the game that night in Camden. The car had to be from The Big Jack, so I found his face in the crowd. He waved and shouted something. I figured he was telling me that the keys were under the visor in the car, and they were.

We pulled away, to a greatly satisfying clatter. A chalet was booked for us down at the Lake – The Big Jack again – but as soon as we were out of sight, Carolyn quietly said, "Can you pull the car over, please?" She threw the door open, her shoulders heaved, then she closed the door. "False alarm." Deep breath. "Let's go to my mom's house for a little while."

Her mother showed up no more than twenty minutes later. One of the neighbors had come over to the wedding and told her this strange car was in her driveway.

-- Is everything all right?

-- She's not feeling well, she's resting right now, I replied.

Her mother went into Carolyn's bedroom.

-- She's asleep.

-- Do you think we should call the doctor?

We talked it over. Her mother wanted to know everything that had happened after we left the wedding.

-- She gets like this sometimes lately, her mother said.

She offered me a drink and poured one for herself. We shared what we had seen of Carolyn during the wedding.

While we were talking, Carolyn opened the door. She was out of her wedding dress and into a sheer white nightgown. She was as pale as the gown. We both jumped up to support her, but she waved us off. She lurched over to the chair nearest the door and collapsed.

"I'm sorry," she said faintly.

Her mother and I spoke simultaneously:

Me: Don't worry about the Lake, just rest.

Mrs. Gaertner: What can I do for you?

Carolyn shook her head. "I'm sorry," she repeated. "Jim, can I sit with you? Help me over to the couch."

On the couch, she put her head on my chest, I put my arms around her, and she was gone again.

About the time it started to get dark, she suddenly woke up. "Why are you here? Don't you have a game tonight?"

"Not me. They gave me the night off. Something about a wedding."

"But it's the Regionals."

"Not for another week. Then I'll have to go, but I'll call every chance I get."

She started to say something and stopped. Finally she murmured, "Thank you. I need you," and was asleep again. Her mother brought a blanket to cover her.

We talked in low voices. She let me know that she had called the Lake to cancel our reservation. I felt Carolyn's forehead to see if she had any fever; she seemed normal. Did she ever eat? I asked, again; I hadn't seen her eating anything except a nibble of the cake. I didn't mention what Mike had said was going on in the ladies' room.

We talked about the car in the driveway. She said, maybe, if I ask, he'll give me a car like that, mine's falling apart. Actually, her car was a year old, but I decided not to mention it.

We talked about putting Carolyn into a bed. Her bed, or her mother's? She might be more comfortable with her mother. On the other hand, this was our wedding night. I was torn, but we decided on her bed and bedroom, and I would stay in the room. I picked Carolyn up while her mom went to find The Big Jack's camping gear so that I could sleep on Carolyn's floor. When I got up later that night, I found her mother asleep in the chair right outside our door.

A few days later, it seemed, she suddenly got bigger. It was almost as if she had willed herself to stay slim until the wedding was past. I was at my parents' house. The arrangement all along had been that she would stay with her mom and I would stay with my folks until the house was ready, and we would take some weekends away for time alone together. But, between basketball and finishing the house, we never did make it to the Lake or anywhere else.

Ah, the basketball. You might remember the end of that season. Most people around here do still remember. When, to the surprise of everyone, we made it through the Regionals and into the Statewide Finals, the hoopla started. We were heroes, the Cinderella team that came from way back in the woods to face schools that had twenty times our enrollment.

Then we won our first state playoff game. The media went crazy: coverage in the big newspapers, interviews on television, even a mention in the Miscellaneous Highlights column of the big national sports magazine.

We were in the State Great Eight. Now we were going to be facing Richmond in the semi-finals. Mighty Richmond. Goliath versus David. Richmond that was nationally ranked, with not one but two players among the High School All-America team. Everyone said the dream is over; Richmond is sure to crush us.

Everyone was right. Richmond crushed us.

We had another surprise when we got home. We were still heroes. We were the plucky, undaunted, resolute, fearless local boys who only succumbed to overwhelming force, but never gave up, never stopped trying, and almost made it. (What game did they see?). For the next few years we were held up as an inspiration to every schoolkid in the Valley.

If you don't remember anything else, you may have heard this saying around Taylor: "Goliath's still out there." It was something from a television interview just before the Richmond game. When the interviewer asked me what I thought of our chances, I answered, "Pretty good, if Goliath isn't there. But he is, isn't he? He hasn't left, has he?"

I said more, of course, but that's the line that people remember. Since then, I've seen that line quoted several times and in various different ways, usually "Goliath's still there," or, "Goliath's still out there, isn't he?" As far as I know, I was the first to say it.

And the college offers *did* improve, even though at my request coach had stopped putting my name out there. (I believe Mike also got an offer or two, but I never asked, and he's never mentioned it.)

The baby came just before we were able to move into the house. Carolyn had an easy delivery. I was able to stay with her. I remember the moment our daughter was born, our daughter!, all red and wet and misshapen, straining to cry. Carolyn smiled weakly. Before I knew it, I was holding the baby. She was so small I could cradle her in one hand.

We named her Erin Josephine, after my grandmother. They sent the baby home to Carolyn's mother while Carolyn stayed in the hospital for a few more days. There'd been a problem with bleeding and a low fever. Even after she was released from the hospital, she had no energy and had trouble eating, but her temperature had returned to normal. The mothers took turns taking care of the baby, and we were moving everything into our house that we would need. Mom made sure I learned what I had to know to take care of Erin.

One morning when I was cutting and tacking the last of the bead trim in what would become the nursery, Carolyn unexpectedly showed up at the nursery door. She looked so much better than she'd looked at breakfast. "It's beautiful," she cried. "Just like I pictured it. I can't wait to see furniture in here."

Two weeks later, she left her mother's house and came home. We were together at last. That night we lovingly tucked the baby in, went to the living room, and shared a glass of red wine. The baby cried. Carolyn was startled. "Jim, can you take care of it? I … I don't have any idea what to do. My mother would never let me do anything."

"It's not tough,' I said. We walked into the nursery, and I picked Erin up. She got quiet right away. To Carolyn, I said, "Here's the deal. She's either tired, or hungry, or dirty, or lonely, like now, or she just wants to cry for no reason. Here's where you'll find all the stuff that you'll need."

Carolyn was a good student and very conscientious, and Erin and she gradually became comfortable with each other. We had a life together. It seemed less and less like Carolyn was playing house. But her eating problems did not completely go away. She had lost the weight from the pregnancy and more.

By then I had work as a carpenter's helper. Once or twice, when I would come home from work, the baby would be crying and Carolyn almost asleep holding her, too weak to do more. Sometimes she would take the baby to her mother's and stay there a day or two.

We talked about having a child of our own. Carolyn thought it was something we should do. We even tried a few times, very uncomfortably.

Around that time her father left the state altogether. He'd accepted an even more lucrative position back on the East Coast. After that, Carolyn often stayed in bed all weekend, and there was no more talk of starting a family. She was barely taking care of the baby we had.

I loved it when Erin began talking, but that's when things really started slipping even further for Carolyn. She would tap me in bed: I think I have to go to the doctor; can you forget work and stay with Erin today? Or can your mother stay with her?

The house had an unfinished room. I finished it with dad's help, so that one of the mothers could stay when necessary. Then the folks said, We don't mind helping, but let's see if we can get Mrs. Beswick to move in.

Mrs. Beswick – Missus B. -- was a childless widow who'd worked with dad at the mill, but they'd cut her hours back. Now, even with some part-time work, she was barely surviving. If she was interested in moving into that bedroom and helping until Carolyn was back on her feet, they would help us financially as much as they could.

So Mrs. Beswick moved in. She would still be there fourteen years later when The Big Jack put Erin into a college prep school in the Midwest.

Now I'm almost as old as Mrs. Beswick was when she first came to us. All this time I've wondered if having her come was the right thing to do. Because when she moved in, Carolyn basically moved out. The move was supposed to be temporary. Mostly she stayed with her mother; she had more time to take care of her swan than we did.

But that didn't work either. Within a few months her weight shot up. She became enormous. Her mother said that we were the perfect 10 as a couple: I was the "1" and Carolyn was the "0."

At first we hoped her weight gain was a baby, but it wasn't; it was alcohol – all those empty calories. We had our share of drinking problems in Taylor, so when we started finding those little bottles whenever she'd be at our house or with my folks, we knew pretty clearly what was happening.

Not a word was said. We just took the bottles that we found and left them on our kitchen table. A week or so later, whenever she visited, the bottles would disappear. But new little bottles kept turning up in the usual hiding places.

It was time for a call to her dad.

I'm guessing there was a stormy session at her house when he came, but I don't know for sure.

I do know that, a month later, she was in a very expensive rehab down in the southwest. Famous people were there; it was embarrassing who I saw. They even had a family program where they provided us with plane tickets so we could be part of family therapy. I couldn't image how much the place must be costing.

She didn't always understand why she was there, but she went to the meetings and otherwise did what they told her to do. Before long, she'd turned the corner; she was clean, and she was losing the weight.

There was still a problem. She kept losing the weight.

The next thing I knew, they'd moved her to the eating disorder wing of the facility. She was much happier there. When I visited, she had a routine. She would show me all her foods, and her written diet, and the checkmarks next to the foods she had eaten, all annotated with the times she had eaten them. (She had an exercise program too, but that didn't go as well.)

She had a special aide – Susan -- who had endless time for her. They spent hours together, going over her charts and reviewing all her checkmarks, making notes and corrections as required. Susan played a ukulele, and they would sing together. She loved going out onto the patio where she could rest in the sun.

One day maybe three months later, she was very excited. "Hey, goose, I'm coming home!" she said. "They told me yesterday that I'm leaving here in a month." She wanted me to bring pictures of the house, and the gardens, and Erin, how big she must be getting. I couldn't bring myself to tell her that, yes, she was leaving, but no, she wasn't coming back to the house. Or maybe she knew that The Big Jack had worked out a program with a local clinic; he would be funding the program so that she could be in it. I promised I would bring her the pictures.

The local clinic was not nearly as fancy as the place in the southwest, but it was also nowhere near as expensive. Even so, I wondered how long The Big Jack could afford supporting a whole program, but he did. Carolyn liked being there, and we all liked being closer.

She was allowed to come home. When she came, she would be full of energy, cheerfully setting about cooking and cleaning and mothering, but she could only go for a few hours before her energy would give out. And, as hard as she tried, she couldn't get comfortable with Erin. Her home visits became less frequent, and finally stopped altogether.

Erin seemed to miss her mother, but when I brought her with me to the clinic, Carolyn often had no interest in her, especially when Erin cried, so I brought her less and less. Instead, I would bring a teddy bear with me and say that it came from Erin, that Erin was thinking of her. And then Carolyn would smile and we would talk home and the old times.

Sometimes when I would go, one of her few friends from school would be there, or I would bring her mother. Her father was of course too busy, but every few days there'd be a new bouquet of flowers from him. She missed her aide from the rehab. We were able to find a volunteer who would go to the clinic once a week to sing with her.

The teddy bears piled up. We talked to the doctor who visited monthly. She went over the test results with us. She was concerned about this level, and that number, but told us that basically Carolyn was in reasonable shape physically; at least I think that's what she was saying. Nevertheless, her energy kept slowly disappearing. She'd long since stopped coming home. She sang less and less. I had tried getting her out to the basketball court at the town park, but she wasn't interested. Her doctor brought in a psychologist.

Finally she was mostly sleeping, and almost never out of the bed. They were feeding her, but without much success. If it wasn't one infection, it was another. But she was always happy to see me.

It was midafternoon in the spring a little over four years after the wedding that the clinic called me. Can you get here right now? Come quickly, she's awake and alert, and she wants to see you.

When I got there, she was gleeful. "Oh, I just had the most terrible thought. Can I share it with you? You won't be angry?" She hid her face in the blanket for a moment, then, "It's really terrible. Promise me you won't take it the wrong way. Promise! Promise! Cross your heart and hope to die?"

I promised.

"Help me sit up."

When she was sitting, she half closed her eyes, lowered her voice. "Ah'm thinkin' mah race hereabouts is startin' tah wind down." I tried to stop her, but she waved me off and continued gleefully. "Ma time is just arunnin' out. They'll be abringin' the bucket b'fore long. Ah'm agonna be headed on up tuh that last big roundup. So I guess there's no harm any more in telling you now, I mean, lettin' yuh know who done it. Identifyin' the feller. It don't matter nohow ennymore ennyway." Stagy **cough cough** "It was ..” **cough cough** “It was .. “ **cough cough** Suddenly she flung her arms out in wild alarm and cried out “BANG!”

She fell back dead on the pillow, giggling uncontrollably, her arms across her shriveled chest.

I couldn’t help myself; I was giggling too. I had to. Even across the years I knew this game so well. I also knew that she was telling me goodbye. She was telling me goodbye in the best way she could and expecting me to do my best as well.

“Is that too terrible? No? See,” she blurted, “You can still laugh. I can still make you laugh.” She waited expectantly.

My turn. I did do my best. “Now we’ll never know. She’s gone. And I’m too late. If only I hadn’t taken the time to stop to get that teddy bear.”

She whispered, “Not important. Do you haf ze plans, kamerad?”

“No, but, my goodness, you must be the pretty new schoolteacher. Without your glasses, you’re beautiful.”

“Oh, Ashley, you always do say the kindest things. Could you just step over there for a moment and get me one more little sip of that delicious punch?”

“It’s no use,” I replied, “the car won’t start. Maybe they’ll let us call for help from that beat-up overgrown old mansion up on that hill over there.”

“But suppose he has a neutralizer?”

“No problem. You, you watch the door. While you do that, I’ll take care of the teller. Max here will wait outside with the car.”

“White man speakum with straight tongue?”

“Of course. And Dr. Laura here will also be joining us on the expedition.”

“So we make camp here? I’ll tell the others.” She’d closed her eyes.

Yes, I thought, we’ll make camp here. “Are you getting tired?”

“Just a little. It’s all right. Those were the days, weren’t they?”

“Yes, they were,” I agreed.

The ceiling fan went woop … woop … woop. The world outside the door had dropped away. It was getting late.

“So,” she sighed. “Remember the fish. Those big fish? At the bridge?”

I did. When we were kids, they used to take us down to the Lake. There was a bridge over the stream that flowed out of the

Lake where we loved to watch the fish. Dad pointed out that all the big fish were on one side of the bridge but not on the other, He said it was because you could fish all the way beyond the bridge, but fishing was not allowed in the short section between the Lake and the bridge. Somehow the fish knew it. On the far side of the bridge there were no fish at all. On the Lake side, the fish were enormous, swimming around in slow, big circles.

She was saying something I could barely hear. ".. the day it rained so .." And with that she drifted away.

As much to myself as to her, I said, "Why don't you rest? I'll come see you later," and left as quietly as I could.

Halfway down the corridor, the torrents came, far enough away that she wouldn't see me or hear me. I couldn't stop myself. Then I was screaming with all my might, but soundlessly. I could do that by then. One does learn certain skills.

Then somehow I was outside, wiping my eyes so that I could find the car and go home.

She was there for another month or so, mostly sleeping. Sometimes she would be half awake, her eyes barely open, and she would smile when she saw I was there. Her lips would move, sometimes whispering, sometimes soundless, but I couldn't understand her, so I would just rest my hand on hers, and she would close her eyes with the smile still on her lips.

One day her pillow seemed damp. I went out to the desk and mentioned it, and a few minutes later an aide came and changed the pillow.

A few nights later I got a call. Come now, they said. She wants you.

At the desk her aide Emily told me that Carolyn had been half awake briefly, crying for me, whispering my name. She's asleep now but go in, she might wake up again.

She was breathing steadily, but very faintly. This might be it, I thought. I touched her hand. Then I did for the first time what I have done so often since then when I thought someone was ready to go. I tell them that they could move on now if they want to. We will be all right on this side until we all meet again on the other. I asked her to remember me to all the people who had gone before. I said a prayer over her. I told her how Erin was talking now, and how much Erin loves her, and how big she was getting, and what a big little helper Erin was, how she had been helping Mrs. Beswick cook breakfast that morning.

An aide I did not know came in to take her pulse.

"Is she there?"

"She's still there. It might be awhile. Could be hours. Or more."

The aide left, and we were alone again. I'm sure I repeated most of what I had said -- Erin, the house, my work, the weather, Mike's latest car. If I could find a book, even a paperback, I could read to her, keep comforting her with words. But what I found in the bedside drawer was a Bible. A list of passages was written on the inside front cover.

The first was from Paul. I found it. He said, *"The peace of God, which transcends all understanding, will guard your hearts and your minds in Christ Jesus."* I whispered the words, as if I might wake her if I said them any louder.

She was so still, so calm. Her battle was over. She was going home. A-headin' home.

The next was Paul again. I've since found that Paul does that, he sticks to you. *"Neither death nor life, neither angels nor demons, neither the present nor the future, nor any powers, neither height nor depth, nor anything else in all creation, will be able to separate us from the love of God that is in Christ Jesus our Lord."*

I was in no hurry. The halls were quiet. Every so often a nurse or an aide went past the door. Every so often I could barely detect distant conversation, the low murmur of words.

"Because of the LORD's great love we are not consumed, for his compassions never fail. They are new every morning; great is your faithfulness."

It seemed like she was still breathing. I couldn't be sure.

"Peace I leave with you; my peace I give you. I do not give to you as the world gives. Do not let your hearts be troubled and do not be afraid." I repeated that one, and then again. Then I told her how peaceful it was in this room, how everything from here on would be peace, how the rest of us could only envy the peace that now surrounded her, filled her, sustained her, lifted her onward.

We were all part of the flow – Carolyn, all the other people who had passed and would pass through this room, and all the times since then that I've been there with someone as they passed. One day, my turn would come. In this same room, if I had anything to say about it. Someday someone would read these verses over me.

"So do not fear. Do not fear, for I am with you."

The ceiling fan circled lazily.

"He that sitteth on the throne shall dwell among them. They shall hunger no more, neither thirst anymore; neither shall the sun light on them, nor any heat. For the Lamb which is in the midst of the throne shall feed them and shall lead them unto living fountains of waters: and God shall wipe away all tears from their eyes."

When I had run out of the verses that were listed, I started repeating them. It just seemed like the right thing to do. I thought, suppose it does take days? Well, then, I'll have had some practice. Now, a few days from now, all the same.

Around that time the room started to get light. It seemed to me that her breathing, that steady faint rise and fall, had disappeared, but I kept right on. All I wanted was every possible moment with her. The halls were quiet, and nothing was moving yet outside: no cars, no birds, nothing.

The same aide came in and took her pulse. "She's gone."

I signed some papers at the desk. To me they were just wet paper. I don't remember crying. I thought I was all out of tears.

Tuesday, December 16

Did it. Did my writing and got it outta here. Now what? How do I feel now? Not sure, but I think right now I don't feel anything at all. Not much sleep again last night and more terrible mixed up vague crazy dreams when I did sleep.

Did get a welcome distraction in the mail, an invite to something called the Roanoke Ecumenical Clergy Convention. Nice paper, all engraved-looking, and some potentially interesting topics, particularly this Church Without Walls. But it's a long ride, and I'm not getting any younger, or any richer, and I don't need most of the other topics: New Ideas in Stewardship. Building Our Congregations. Current Compensation Packages and Benefits. Recruiting Strategies for Mission Trips. Getting and Retaining Church Officers. Revitalization. I couldn't help thinking, If we're not asking the right questions, the answers aren't important. So what are we going to do? Keep breathing. Celebrate the small victories. And, hey, maybe a new idea. It could happen. But don't go overboard.

Thinking about Hal too. Where do we go from here? I don't see where I'll ever get him into a church. I'm thinking we could read together, if it's not called 'reading.' I see him already as being born again from what he was. Well, being born the first time takes months, and then years. And in its own time. So also for the second time around. Give him time. Give me time.

Hold this thought: Servant heart.

Wednesday, December 17

Had a dream, made a decision, went to see Mac down the road at the travel agency. A little travel is a good thing, so they say. Putting off work for a few; called my people to explain, and they seemed to understand.

Talked with Mac about Jack and Mike in St. Guayábe and what they were doing there. I told him how we'd sold the Fiat and that Mike would be working on a new car but wasn't quite sure what it was. He said to tell him about it as soon as I found out..

Oh, yes, the plane tickets. On to St. Guayábe. He'll get back to me by Friday. Do you need a car or a hotel? Just asking. As to the tickets, these last-minute trips always cost, he warned me. He'll try to find a deal, but no promises.

Still thinking about Jonah, he who tried to escape God and ended up in the belly of a whale. A great fish. Am I escaping God in the silver belly of a great plane? Guess I'll find out. Maybe finding out is part of His plan.

All quiet at the clinic, thank goodness. After all that writing, I wasn't eager to see any hospital action for a while. And how it was Carolyn being there that got me started going to the clinic, and so on.

Called Jack and told him I was coming after all. He always knew that I'd weaken. He wanted to know what had kept me. You're still the same, he said. The Great Equivocator. But it's all right. The place is all set up for you, and everything is taken care of. You'll be right at home. Hey, you already missed the Great Seagull Fight. Seems this kumquat brought fish chunks or something out from the mainland to feed the pelicans, but the seagulls came swarming around him instead. There were so many of them, in the guy's face and nipping at his hand, that he dropped the bag and ran, and the seagulls fought over it for about twenty minutes. When they finally were done, all that was left was a few shreds of bag and a lot of poop. You know, he said, wrapping up the thought, 'it reminded me of that time at the bargain counter at the department store that me and Ann had gone to years ago, one of the times we went below to do our Christmas shopping.'

Never did manage to get a word in about why I'm going, about the accident. He said Mike hasn't come in yet but is talking about me.

Got to thinking on that 'Great Equivocator' crack and what I just wrote about Carolyn. I was so much more sure of myself when we first came together than I am now. But that was never really me; that was just someone doing like they do in the movies. Once she started getting really sick, those movies weren't much help anymore.

Thursday, December 18

Busy with the day nowadays, maybe have time when I get there, or maybe wait until I get back.

Went down to see Morrie at the *Trumpet.* No problem with sending him St. Guayábe stuff if I want to.

Then to the gym, shot my last hoops for a while. Several of the kids wished me safe travels, wanted to know when I'd be back. Gave the Gerrity boys a copy of my workout notes, so they'll be able to practice their drills without me. They're all a good bunch this year, I'll miss 'em.

"I'll miss 'em?" That sounds funny. I'm probably only gone a week.

Jack's told Rosey about me coming, says Rosey's looking forward to me being there, wants to talk scripture with me. Do I preach the Five Square Bible? Or the Bible of Jubilee Coming? The Bible of Bliss? He hopes I don't preach the Bible of His Fiery Wrath.

Serious? Kidding? Not to worry, saith Jack, Rosey wants to meet me, hear the Word, says I can preach any Bible I want. Wants to know if I can do a service out there, maybe a service for Christmas or Christmas eve?

And I should know that he's created a new drink to honor my presence in his modest establishment -- the Jimbo Bombo.

Then Jack got nervous, had something he wanted to say, but wasn't sure how to say it. Seems they had a little contest at Rosey's last night. It's a contest they have every month on the night farthest from the full moon. Seems it's a challenge for the ladies. Seems that, if they're willing to run topless from the bar down to the water and back, they get free drinks for the rest of the night. But Jack reassured me, said not to worry. First, if I ever saw them running, I would not be tempted. Completely the opposite, in fact. You never saw such flying you-know-what's in your life. Hard even to look. And also, you won't be here that long, it won't come along for another month, and you'll only be here for a week. Unless he runs an unscheduled race.

Mike says hello, totally beat but can't wait to see me, eager to show me what he's working on, wants to surprise me.

Nothing from Hal yet.

From today's *Strumpet*, courtesy me:

Funny! Funny!

Thanks to long-time reader Phil Ormsby over in Pine Hill for pointing out that the specifications for the Syracuse crane printed in last week's rag -- namely, Jupiter 4-4-0 with 16" x 24" cylinders and 5' driving wheels, a weight of 65,450 lbs. and approximately 11,500 pounds of tractive effort – have nothing to do with the crane at the school but are actually the specifications for the famed Jupiter railroad engine from the 1860's that participated in the transcontinental railroad Golden Spike ceremony at Promontory Point. It appears that our Foreman Saltzer has a bubbling sense of humor – he certainly hoaxed yr. humble scribe!

Friday, December 19

Can't concentrate. What does he think of what I sent him? Too much? It would be *really* nice to see him.

Mildred's fine. Both of them are clueless, even with the suitcase open on the couch. Jack says his dog went crazy when his suitcases came out. Ann taking the cats – did I mention that before? – says she might just want to keep the cats and send Jack over to me when all this is done but asked what I've heard from him lately.

Asked Jack about Mike's car – what's this big surprise? He doesn't know, but he'll find out.

Finally got some sleep. No big dreams, not even Carolyn dreams. Down deep I must finally be at peace with this, or maybe just distracted with all the preparations. Wish I had the tickets in my hand now; I'll get them tomorrow.

Saturday, December 20

Still busy. Busy, busy. Made another decision . Mac had said, no two-stop flight available until Tuesday. He had put together a three-stop flight for tomorrow, if I'm interested. Long trip: down to 'La Capitol,' then from this capitol to some place called Juárez de la Pantera, and then a puddle jumper from there to New Hampton, but not into the big modern new airport; instead into the municipal airport. Costs more, a few pennies; less comfortable. Looks pretty much primitive actually. Want to wait? No matter, I said, book it. It's a long, uncomfortable trip no matter how I do it.

So I have the tickets, need to let Jack know about the change in airports. Any port in a storm for me at this point.

Odd package in the mail today, the Roanoke people again. Can't quite figure it out – it looks like they want me to present?! Or be on a panel? How did they ever find me? No matter, I'll have to figure it out when I get back.

[Later] Jack called early; says it'll be hot tomorrow. No problem with the change in airport. In fact it's better – about 20 miles less driving, and I'm there sooner, and it'll be that much easier to find me in the local airport.

They had a big storm down there the other night: rain, wind, sounded like standing under a plane taking off. House shook. Jack said he thought the end had come. Next day the lady next door is out there cleaning up the mess. Jack said, what did you think of the storm last night? There was a storm? said she and asked if he cared to come in for a spot of tea and biscuit. So now he knows all about her terrarium, her late husband, the tea set that was her mother's. Get this, she even has a cat.

Mike says hello, through Jack, still can't wait to show me what he's working on.

[Still later] Nothing doing at Willow Camp. She wasn't there. Nothing doing there, no feelings at all. Maybe this is how I lose my life to gain it? Whatever. Whatever it is, let's just get on with it, please.

[Later later] Sitting out here on the lawn chair, watching the stars over the ridge. Won't see that again for a few. Getting chilly of nights, but at least no snow. Yet. (Tonight -- chilly! Tomorrow – chili!) Let's see. Cats gone. Cash? Yes. Saw Mrs. Beswick, she's fine, needs nothing. Suitcase at door –those catalogs for Mike, a quickie bag, and last-minute notes from Jack to drop off for Little Mike. Last minute notes for me too. Binder of St. Guayábe notes. Mail stopped. Tickets. Passport. Guide. Money. For the airport, change for snacks. Books to read. Definitely some time to do some thinking.

No problems once I get to St. Guayábe, they've got it covered. Nice place, I'll like it. All taken care of.

Cats gone. Are they missing me? Doubtful. When I dropped them off with Ann, she asked me if I was all right. Remember to thank her. Carolyn, gone too. Or taking her with me? Guess we'll find out when we get there. Nice to see my friends. Guess it's a good idea. Jonah plus whale = Jim plus plane? I hope not. Go to bed please.

Sunday, December 21

Otherwise, everything set. Hoping I didn't forget anything. Funny here without Mabel and Mildred, but excited. Dark out there. Long day ahead. Houseplants gone, took them over to the car wash, hoping Little Mike remembers to water them. Didn't find anyone for the birdfeeders, so figuring the birds will just have to wing it for a week. Anyway, time to go. Go, man, go.

Servant heart? Wish I knew. He's got some plan, it's all for a reason, I'll find out when I get there. He trusts me, I just have to trust more, too. Maybe the point of the exercise? Feels right, or, in any case, better – different? -- than staying here. One, two, three – leap!

New Every Morning

Let's just forget about that chaos at the airport. We'll just sit down here and do this thing for Morrie, right, Mr. James?

New Hampton, St. Guayábe
December 23
Jim Lawrence
Words: 618

They tell me that this tiny sliver of Caribbean real estate is a tropical paradise, and I believe them. They speak of gentle breezes and soft sands, riotously colorful masses of flowers hanging in baskets, soothing strains of steel drum music wafting in the dense air, dim and noisy markets teeming with exotic fruits, lingering traces of the fabled buccaneers of so long ago, stories of buried treasure and arrrgh walk the plank. All this must be true of this tropical paradise called St. Guayábe, in Central America, far from our familiar surroundings.

But so far yr. humble scribe hasn't seen it.

What I have seen so far is an airport that looks very much like Bedford County Airport minus the drag racing (we're working on it!); the marbled town square of their capital city, New Hampton, that humbles our town square in Taylor; and this cozy two-bedroom suburban stucco domicile where we are staying near the town square, with its kitchen stacked with dirty dishes and this breezy porch overlooking the very image of our well-tended grassy lawns back home. Even this: our ancient 'Jack's Lawn Care' van parked in the driveway here.

And did I mention that our cozy cottage in New Hampton is located on Taylor Street? *Taylor Street?* Yes, Taylor Street.

So, I sit here of the morning, having polished off my breakfast of sausage omelet and ice-cold, ice-cubed diet soda. Next door, our neighbor has come out on her porch to sip her tea. We wave to each other. Two doors down, a man in his pajamas walks his dog under a streetlight. Might I be forgiven for thinking I've never left home?

True, some things are different. At home we rest in a valley and look up to the mountains. Here I rest on a hillside high above the dark ocean, which is fringed with dim alluring islands that slowly brighten as the sun rises behind a streak of clouds in the far distance.

And the birds are different here. They don't have many kinds of birds here, but, when they do have birds, they have *birds!* A whole bunch of birds. Masses of birds. At this moment, a swirling, chattering mob of these tiny yellow fellows called 'bananaquits' has arrived. These bananaquit birds love sugar. A small cup filled with sugar crystals on the porch railing is what is drawing them here; anywhere from thirty to fifty of these bananaquits are crowded around the cup or flitting about, waiting their turn or diving in to get their daily dose of goodness.

And, for our local history buffs, I might note that our Taylor is actually different from their Taylor. Our Taylor, as every local schoolchild will be happy to remind us, is Zachary Taylor, hero of the Mexican American War and subsequently President of these United States. Their Taylor here in New Hampton, it turns out, is named for his son, Richard, who fought for the Confederacy in the Civil War. In fact, all the streets in our subdivision here – Stirling Price Gardens -- are named for generals from the old Western Confederacy. Besides Taylor and Price, there's Shelby, Hindman, Polk, Magruder, and the rest. The Confederacy is still a very big deal down here – more on that later.

As I write, the sun is poking above those dim islands, now etched against a sea washed with gold. The town below is quiet in the early morning air. Soon I'll be heading down there, to see what I can see. There are errands to run, a special parade car to look at, an ancient cathedral to visit, and a daylight stroll to view the historic square and its surrounding stately government offices.

And then? Perhaps a sunset sail across the lagoon to wrap up the day? Maybe this place might not be quite like home after all.

I read over what I had written. Not terrible, I thought. Certainly, it was picturesque and upbeat, sunny, very optimistic. It certainly captured the idea that I wanted to capture: This place could be our America. So far.

But I wasn't sure. What I'd written was the truth, up to a point. The view from the porch *is* stunning. The lawn *is* green. The lady next door *did* come out to drink her tea.

But it wasn't quite the whole truth. I'd said, "Maybe this place might not be like home after all." Really? Should I totally ignore the fracas at the airport with Jack and some lady friend of his, and then how Mike and I spent half the night getting Jack out of jail? Am I crazy? Why am I writing this stuff?

But it's done, Mr. James. And you need to get this out now. We'll have plenty of chances to develop the story later. And there's no way I can say anything about the airport fracas anyway. In the meantime, do it. Do the cover letter, find a place to buy stamps and mail it, get it out of here, and get on with your time here. Just do it. And a postcard for Erin and the folks back home.

Do another Institute report as soon as you've seen Mike.

Do the cover letter now:

Hey, Morrie, greetings & Merry Merry from yr. humble scribe here in St. Guayábe. Here's my first-impressions scribble, just like you wanted, hope you like it. I'm realizing I'll probably be back before this thing hits the street (did we think about that? – I'm only here a week!), assuming you use it, so feel free to change it around – maybe a line of explanation or change it to something along the lines of "They told me .." Your call, as always.

There's going to be a lot more to this place than just this one article – as much as you can stand. Today I'm on my way over to see the new race car that Mike Charney is building up for the parade – story there, and for next spring too. Talk about the parade? Probably better if we stick with the car, I think Mike's not done with his idea when he gets back to the Valley.

From there I go to St. Anselm, their old historic cathedral, and then over to this place – probably a bar --that they call 'Rosey's World Peace & Love Shack' – definitely should get something from all of that.

Leaving out our little adventure already – yes, we had one but I'm not sure it's printable (need to research those libel laws!) -- so will tell you about it when next we meet. Suffice to say we're all safe and sound now. Of course Jack Van Dorn and Mike Charney send regards. Now to mail this screed as enclosed, and keep moving. Ever fond regards as always and seasoned greetings from yr. humble scribe.

In the distance below, a small boat – a fishing boat? a yacht? – had set out from the marina and was crossing the harbor toward those islands now washed in sunlight. I watched it go – assured, perky -- and thought that I could hear its throbbing engine, but it was just too far away.

From here it was all so serene. I already knew it was not so serene once one left our little haven on the hill. Aside from that small matter of Jack in jail last night, there was the rather larger suspicion that this spot of home around us, probably old military housing?, was set in a larger sea of something else down there which was most definitely not like home.

Mike had said something along those lines. When we arranged to meet at his garage today, he told me I'd have no problem walking around or through New Hampton, but his garage was in the part of town called Canaltown, and I probably should not walk that far. I should look for a cab in the town center or at the cathedral plaza. The guidebook had given similar advice, but in somewhat stronger language: "The area between the town center and the cathedral is safe by day, but visitors are advised not to continue unescorted any farther down the hill at any hour."

And yet the view from the porch was so peaceful.

I read my article over once more. Should I have waited to write? Should I send the article at all? Should I just start over, with a little more of that penetrating insight our readers had come to expect from the *Trumpet*? Had I made allowances to change my tone in my next article if necessary? Yes, I had, there, in that last sentence: "Maybe this place might not be quite like home after all." That was what I needed. Or, at least, it would have to do. Certainly *no* need to tell all of Taylor about our other little adventures.

That's when I decided definitively not to wait for Jack to wake up and drive me to find the post office. A walk into town would work much better, would give me a chance to think our adventures through, put them in place, get a grip on myself, and get a better look at this place. So I stuffed the envelope and set forth.

On the way down the hill toward the town center, I did not want to meet the man walking his dog. I kept going, holding my envelope tightly, eyes straight ahead, not seeing a thing, determined to mail the article before I did anything else. I was concerned – maybe obsessed – with finding the post office and buying the absolute right stamp in the absolute correct amount to put on my envelope, and which corner did the stamp go on, and would the U.S. Postal Service accept it when it reached the States?

uh, Mr. James, that's not why we're taking this little walk.

stop look around uh, that's why we're walking

I'd reached the bottom of the hill. Ahead of me was a wall, with masses of flowers tumbling over the top. A large black spider scurried for cover. A lizard was clinging to the brick, just hanging there, totally immobile, for maybe thirty seconds. Suddenly, tiny legs windmilling, it bolted across the wall, slipped, tumbled to the cobblestone below, and disappeared into the floral debris.

What differences? I thought.

Come on now, I'd written the article. Now .. just .. send .. it. Suppose it's all wrong? Then I'll fix it. Back in Taylor they won't know anyway. *How could I write what I wrote?* Doesn't matter. Sheer habit probably. Do the work first, Mr. James, right? So mail it and move on. Next, what was it you promised we'd do on this walk? Something about thinking?

I wished I were already at the town square, where I could sit on one of the benches we'd seen last night, but I wasn't. I wanted to make notes, form up a list, like little soldiers on the page. What do I do when I'm overwhelmed? I can master this. I've been overwhelmed before. So, Mr. James, what do you do? He thinks of just one thing at a time, that's what Mr. James does. He thinks of one thing at a time. So that's what I'll do.

I *won't* think about the Richmond game (where did *that* come from?). Or Carolyn. Or Hal, who didn't call again after the final Carolyn piece. Or Jack, who I'm not sure I'm speaking to at the moment .. or .. STOP!

One thing please. Something small enough to be contained, but big enough to contain.

That's good, I like that. Nice flow of the sounds. 'Contained,' 'contain.' Now how do I improve it?

No. Should I just open this envelope up and trash the whole article? Or fix it? But how to fix it? Just rip it up and toss it? Then what do I have for an article?

stop

okay, i'm stopped

so you're stopped. But keep walking, dimwit.

Too late. Uh, oh, here comes the avalanche … that airport mad scene, the flight, Jack and me and Mike, waiting for Jack, Hal .. Carolyn .. the status report I owe .. will we ever hear back? .. what am I doing here? .. the money .. parade car – dragster? dragster .. cathedral .. Jonah .. dirty dishes .. am I lost? .. will this article get to Morrie in time .? Jack .. is Jack mad? .. am I mad? .. this Rosey .. have to go to this Rosey and do a Christmas service .. Christmas eve? .. Bombo .. please make that a 'Jimbo Bombo' .. and what's so dangerous about Canaltown? .. what am I doing here? .. I should go to Rosey's today even if I have to skip the cathedral .. I need to talk to Jack, I don't want to talk to Jack .. *jail* .. hate jails .. no ministry for me there, just hate them, trapped .. how are the cats, do they miss me? .. and the cathouse, out behind StateLine, and the guy at Stumpy's who went with the woman at the bar .. that's not me, I'm good .. sure I am .. always do right, Mr. James, it's better that way .. stand up straight – stop slouching! .. am I running for City Council next fall or not? Or is it Board of Supervisors? .. am I running? .. still running? running from..? .. am I lost? huh, am I lost yet?

STOP!

Airport. Let's do nothing else but airport. Get that done. Get it behind me. Get something done.

I turned to look up the road I'd just come down. Never get up that hill in the snow, I thought. But of course it doesn't snow here. What would that be like?

… yes, our little airport adventure. Let's not. Let's wait until we get to the town square. Get this thing mailed, and then we can find a bench, settle ourselves down and see if we can get all this straight. Listening there, Mr. James?

I found myself, literally, on the steps outside that same police station. The letter was gone, and a card to Erin likewise.

We had been here before, Mike and I, only seven hours ago, sitting right over there at the curb in Jack's van, wondering in the darkness if we were wasting our time, not knowing what happened and what was going to happen.

And talking.

Talking about home.

Talking a lot about the car that Mike is building for the parade. I finally got the story. They're building a dragster, sure, but it's for kids. It's still a rail job, flexible like a full-sized one, but not as long, with the tiny wheels at the front and the fat tires in back. As soon as this one is finished, they'll build another one, and then they'll show them off in the Old Confederate Parade.

Talking about the guy Mike is working with at his garage -- Mr. Ruiz -- wait until you meet him. When he's not working on cars, he's a preacher, like you.

And talking in the darkness about Mike's plan. He would not be coming back to Taylor with us at the end of the week. He would stay until the dragster they were working on was done, but he would come back from time to time to see how Little Mike was doing and fix whatever Little Mike couldn't. He would do that. We had the money for that, right? When this car was done, then they would build another. As he said, what good is one dragster? Both these cars were already sold, and their boss Frenchy from the main garage said he thought he could sell at least four more, right off. But he needed the catalogs, for those tires and for a real engine, so could I be sure to bring them tomorrow?

Talking about what had happened at the airport, which is what had brought us to this place, at three o'clock in the morning, outside a police station, next to an empty town square. Trying to piece it all together

All Mike knew was that he and Jack were waiting for me when a woman Mike did not know burst into the waiting area and walked quickly over to Jack. There you are, are you leaving now? she said, or something like that, sat down next to them and started talking about yoga, a yoga studio. Jack was calm, polite. He excused himself to go to the men's room. When he didn't come back was when she broke down, threw her purse against the floor, and was pounding on the door of the men's room when the police arrived.

Then the plane landed, and, after a while, one of the policemen went out. When he returned, he brought the passengers, and Jack was with you.

I couldn't add much. We couldn't get off the plane right away. Finally we were allowed off, after one of our passengers began raving about the heat. A stout policeman in sweat-drenched fatigues was leading us toward the terminal, a building about the size of one of Jack's carwashes, when suddenly Jack himself fell half backwards out of a window, froze momentarily, and then came over when the policeman motioned for him to join our group.

And then I thought of going inside to the main desk at the police station every hour and being rebuffed, again and again, until the lawyer they called got there, took all the cash we had on us, and told us to stay outside in the van while he took care of everything.

And then waiting again outside while the lawyer did whatever he did, drifting toward sleep until something broke the quiet – a streetlight buzzed, a scooter buzzed around the square, some large insect buzzed outside the van window.

Then I was being jostled awake as Mike got into the van on one side, and Jack got in on the other. On the five-minute car ride back to the house, Jack couldn't stop talking. He told us everything that had happened at the airport, which was pretty much a rehash of what I had seen and what Mike had told me. He speculated on why 'that chickie' was so upset. He wanted to know why it had taken us so long to get him out of jail and why those kumquats had made him wait until two thirty in the morning to let him out. He was still raving at Mike when I went to bed.

And I remembered the woman. How oddly she was dressed: loose colorful outfit, many beads and pendants, golden bracelets, a large floppy straw hat. The scent of her perfume, from the small, shattered bottle near her feet, and the other litter from her purse, and her purse. I remembered how she couldn't stop crying when the policemen let me sit with her to try to comfort her. And I couldn't forget, when they led her and Jack away, how she glanced back and tearfully mouthed a Thank You, and her frightened look.

Anything else? Are we done? Is it gone? Settled? Can we look around now? Deep breath. Breathe.

I took a look around in daylight at the place where we had sat for all those long dark hours.

In front of me the town square was very much like our town square back in Taylor, but grander, with its low colonnaded marble border gleaming white in the early morning sun. Blooms cascaded from baskets suspended from hooks on the streetlights. A streetsweeper went by in front of me, a swishing dance. It had an endless job, what with the litter, the ripeness of the manure at the curb, the sharpness of the constantly growing and constantly dying vegetation.

A flatbed truck loaded with vendors' carts had pulled up across the street. The driver climbed out and went up the stairs I was sitting on, into the station. A few minutes later, he returned, and he and his helper started unloading the carts.

By now businessmen, administrators, whatever they were, with bowler hats and tailored suits and carrying umbrellas, were stepping out of their chauffeured cars to ascend into the stately buildings around the square. An attractive young woman in a flowered dress stopped to talk to a vendor, a balloon seller, then dashed across the street and up the stairs of the courthouse about half a block away. Nurses in white uniforms were going into a gleaming modern structure totally unlike the other buildings. Zoning, right? Zoning is important.

As I sat, I gradually became aware that the steps I was sitting on were not cold. They weren't marble at all. What about those columns up there? I'd admired these broad and stately stairs, the columns with their flowery capitals, the high arched wooden doors, the simple but elegant words chiseled into the frieze above this porch: "We Also Serve." But, when I went up and checked them – knock, knock – the columns weren't marble either. What about the other buildings here – the courthouse, the offices, the governor's mansion, those elegant Georgian apartments?

A horse and carriage had pulled up to the curb, ready to take tourists around the square and the high town. Bicycles were passing. There were streetcar tracks in the cobblestone pavement, but no streetcar yet.

By now I was calmer. A vendor selling Italian ices was leaning against the balustrade, smoking a cigarette while he waited for a customer. I watched him for a while, and the vendor selling the balloons, and the old woman with her flowers.

Let's review the next part of today's adventures, I thought, and pulled out my guide. There was still nothing in the index for Canaltown, but I reread what they had about the cathedral. When I put the guide back into my pack, I saw my notebook in there, but decided not to pull it out yet. Morrie could wait. I'd already taken care of him. The sun was warming me nicely. I knew from what Mike had said that Canaltown would be hot and humid, but there was no sense of it here yet. Maybe later in the day.

I was watching the balloon vendor. No one else was buying yet. He didn't look around. He didn't smoke. He didn't do anything with his balloons. He didn't move, except once to rub his nose. On an impulse I pulled out my notebook and wrote:

> He was an old man and he had not sold a balloon in 37 minutes.
>
> For the first ten minutes, the boy was with him, but he had sent the boy away because he was no longer selling balloons as he once did. He remembered when he used to sell many balloons. That was in the days before. Now he was old, and no one wanted balloons.
>
> In those days there was money. He and the boy would go to the seller of Italian ices. The ices were in the style of New York.
>
> The old man had been to New York. He remembered New York. The women were beautiful there, with long thin legs and bright jewelry. They did not look at him. They did not look at him when he was a city councilman. When he played center field for the great New York *equipo* of baseball, they still did not see him. Even after, when he had much work as a model for cigarette ads, they did not look at him.
>
> Then there was no more work. The craggy look is out, they said. You are too short. You are too tall.
>
> Then the money was gone, and he had to leave the great city.
>
> Now he sold balloons here in the park. But he had not sold a balloon in 39 minutes.
>
> The tall thin man sat on the steps of the police station and watched him, watched the seller of balloons. Should I buy a balloon, the man wondered. What would I do with such a balloon?

Ah, I'm losing it, I thought, and closed my scrapbook. How much of this can you do? Well, we did all right with it, for a while anyway. Try someone else, I thought, but I couldn't come up with another victim to parody. Can't do the Russian writers. Not sure I can even spell those Russian names. How about Poe? Poe in the style of a department store ad? Try: "Quoth the raven, nevermore will you see prices this low on mattresses and bedding!" That's not quite right. Something's wrong. Check it? What's the rest of it? Must be a library around here somewhere.

An orderly group of young girls in tailored blue and white uniforms passed by wordlessly in formation on their way to school. Where are the boys?

A streetcar pulled up. A streetcar. I'd read about them but I'd never seen one.

This one was something like an open bus, or maybe like one of these jitneys that they have down here but so far I'd only seen them in the pictures. Those wooden seats gleamed with varnish. The poles shined. Does this contraption go fast enough to throw you off? Is that why you need those poles? It looked like one of those cable cars in the pictures of San Francisco.

Those seats looked comfortable too, more comfortable than these steps. I thought, I'll go sit over there. I'll take this ancient flying carpet wherever it goes. With luck, it will take me toward Mike's.

The motorman must have gotten off. I never noticed him -- her? -- getting off, but these things don't run by themselves.

And then I was settled on the seat, quite exhilarated. The car sat, throbbing faintly. Not like a bus at all. A bus doesn't have flags and pennants. A bus smells of fumes. This thing was pulsing, and fragrant – the smell of flowers, maybe coming from the park?

On the other hand, a plane is a bus, a bus with wings. Noisy. Smelly. Cramped. Hard. Alien.

All behind me now. Here we have flowers and exhaust fumes, balloons, dignified gentlemen carrying umbrellas, deep varnish. There's no place I need to be and nothing I need to do for another two hours. When was the last time I'd had that experience in my life? There's no place I need to be at this moment. And I thought, here's something that's different. Me. This isn't me, exactly. I'm light. When have I been light? I'm not weighed down with a heavy burden. Was I back then? I must have been. Well, consider this. No obligations or responsibilities. Board of Supervisors? Who needs that? No Carolyn. No Erin. No Erin? I didn't like that, the 'No Erin,' but here it was.

Let it go, Mr. James. Just look around. Take it in. Let it happen. We won't be here long. Be back home in a week.

So what is this place, this square, with its fine marble buildings that aren't marble, and the scooters, and the fountain that isn't working, and this streetcar that doesn't move? What else was I going to find? What would Mike's garage be like, and his neighborhood, and his parade race car? Would this Rosey's place be as special as Jack made it out to be? What about this Christmas service I was supposed to be doing there? At least there would be no snakes; it didn't seem like I would have time to get very far out of town in the few days I would have here.

Around that time I might have started to drift. It was so relaxing here, and I was tired, fighting sleep after our mostly sleepless night.

At any rate I was vividly remembering the flight. Here was a vast shimmering plain dotted with shrubs. I thought we had a wasteland back home, beyond StateLine, but that was a city compared to this desert I'd flown over yesterday. The flatland swayed and danced in the rising air. Nothing down there, not even ruins -- no broken-down fences, no pole lines, no collapsing walls. No fruit trees marking some long-abandoned homestead. No watercourses or dried out riverbeds. No roads or even rutted tracks. No salt streaks. Just these endless checkerboard shrubs sweeping away to a streak of dazzling black clouds over the distant jagged outline of mountains.

Were those the mountains where the 'bandits' were? I thought of Jack and Mike sitting in their convoy line of cars for hours, waiting as their convoy formed that would skirt those mountains.

What about the native people up there in their jungle forest home? Did they know that they were 'bandits' and 'insurrectionists'? I wondered about their life and if they would be able to keep it. Would I want to go among them and proclaim the good news that they were saved? I wondered how they would feel about being saved and if they would wonder what they were being saved from.

And then I thought about hunger and disease, starvation, sudden ambush from that green thicket, those snakes, and the spiders and ants and chiggers and tarantulas and the trees that were poisonous to the touch. Maybe being saved from all that wouldn't look so bad. Maybe some brave hunter might get the impulse to chuck his poisoned darts, rummage around for a tee and cutoffs and a beat-up hat, toss the loincloth into the bushes, and join the side that has chocolate bars. Maybe one of them was the fellow sitting slumped in his carriage over there, waiting for tourists, or one of the cabbies just down the street.

Maybe one of them was operating this trolley.

Maybe not. Was *anyone* operating this trolley?

It was becoming increasingly apparent that swift movement was not part of the plan here in New Hampton, St. Guayábe. What to do? It was already too late to go home. If I wanted to get to Mike's, I would have to do something eventually. I could start walking toward the cathedral, to get a cab there. If there was a cab there. On the other hand, there are cabs here, a whole line of them.

When I was ready to start moving, I went over.

The first cabbie, when I showed him the directions that Mike had given me, refused to take me.

-- Why not?

The cabbie squinted as he read the directions. He shook his head again and told me to wait here.

So I waited here. How difficult could it be? These were the directions: Go to the far side of the plaza. Find the broad street that runs toward the tower of the cathedral. ("It's the boulevard with the concourse of trees down the middle.") Continue past the cathedral and down the hill into the lower town. At the bottom is a small park and a pillar thing that says Canaltown down the side of it in big letters. Go straight ahead one more block. At the soda machine, turn left and go one half block to the garage with the old cars. As Mike said, "It'll be no more than a quarter mile, probably less."

My reluctant cabbie was arguing and gesticulating with several other cabbies maybe three cabs down the line. After a time, he returned and shook his head. Not today. It was not possible today.

-- But how will I get there?

He pointed to a group of young people standing across the street by motorcycles. Maybe talk to them, he suggested.

I went over.

-- Excuse me, but can you take me to this place? It's a garage. It'll have cars parked out front.

They studied the directions I handed to them.

One young man said,

-- I know that place. That's where Mr. Ruiz is, and the norteamericano?

I nodded. How much? I asked.

-- No problem. Whatever you give me. It's very close.

Just like that, I was on a motorcycle. I couldn't help but remember how Hal, after I'd gotten my motorcycle jacket for

Stumpy's, tried unsuccessfully to take me for a ride on his motorbike.

We scooted along the boulevard under the trees. The houses along the boulevard were exactly as the guidebook had described them: turreted, gabled, lawned, porched enormous piles, multicolored cakelike trim, stained glass windows. One of the houses was unforgettable: Under a Christmas palm, complete with lights and presents, they'd set up a complete living room on their front lawn: chairs, tables, a rug, lamps, fans. Christmas in December in St. Guayábe. Differences? What differences?

Then the ground was dropping off ahead of us. On the right, a large overgrown cemetery. On the left, the tower of the Cathedral of St. Anselm. Actually it was a rather squat brick barn with its tower to the front; not very imposing, but I'd been warned. I remembered that the guidebook had much to say about its history, but nothing about its architectural distinction, only noting that the view from the plaza in front of the church was recommended. As we passed by, I had a glimpse of the cathedral plaza ringed with sawhorses and yellow police barricade tape.

And then the cathedral was behind us.

Here we go, shouted my driver, gunning his engine as we plunged down the hill and around an embankment into the lower town. So this was Canaltown.

My first impression was, 'My goodness,' as my mother might have said. My goodness indeed.

A New Jerusalem

This Canaltown was like nothing I'd ever seen. Here at the bottom of the hill was a boiling cauldron of sound. I could barely hear our motorcycle. Music was coming from everywhere, vendors shouting, engines revving, a distant police siren, and, through the din, a gentle Christmas carol coming from the direction of that holiday tree in the tiny park just ahead of us.

And the colors: the people's clothes, the seller's goods, the posters, banners, flags, awnings, drapes. The buildings themselves were pink, blue, lime green, yellow. (Later I saw buildings striped with several colors and another that was purple.)

The street was surprisingly clean – someone was even sweeping – but the smell! Damp. Pungent. That smell reminded me of the acrid odor at the starting line of a dragstrip.

In the middle of the first block, as we circled around that small park, were palms and pushcarts, a news kiosk, tiny buildings, an obelisk in the center of the park with letters that read 'Canaltown' from top to bottom, even a soft drink dispenser just stuck there on the sidewalk. We swerved between shoppers and narrowly missed a blue and white police scooter that shot out in front of us from the left. Narrow alleys led away into shadow.

Past the park was a wall of people, all crowded into the street, because the sidewalks and curbs were jammed with racks of clothes, fruits and vegetables spread out on trays, furniture, appliances. Even delivery trucks were pulled up onto the curbs, parked; if they'd stayed in the street, the street would have been totally blocked. Masses, bundles, clumps, gobs, beehives of wires hung from every pole. Overhead, wires flowed out in every direction, a net above us.

The driver up at the town square was right. No cab or carriage was going to speed through that mob. It would be faster to walk. Even on the motorcycle we had to dart one way and then another to find tiny openings.

It didn't help that my driver was talking to people as we went. I couldn't hear what he was saying but could guess. Some people stared at me, one shook my hand, and several kids went off running down the street and turning at the corner where I had seen on the directions was the way to Mike's garage.

When I tapped my driver on the back and said I could walk from here, he said, oh, no, stay on the motorcycle; he had to go that way anyway if he wanted to see the racecar. So we bobbed along, a boat carried along on a river of humanity. I relaxed and looked around; I had the time.

This was exhilarating. This is abundant life, overflowing life, life almost without rules. It's freedom. I could see why people might think this place was dangerous; it was everything, and everything includes danger. It's life on the mountainside, where an avalanche could break lose any moment. And I could drink it in, quench myself with it. Of course, when it got to be too much, I could leave. I wondered what it would be like not to be able to leave.

As we went, I saw -

- birds in birdcages

- a heavyset man in a blanket wearing dark glasses and playing the guitar, a cup in front of him

- posters and graffiti. A poster in two languages. The English text read, *They call us aliens, but we are all human!*

- women carrying babies

- women dressed modestly, carrying purses and shoulder bags

- women, heavily made up, wearing short pants and tight tops

- boys wearing tee shirts

- boys wearing sports jerseys with team logos

- men dressed like me: slacks, blazers, even some with ties

- the buildings themselves, what I could see of them, seemingly stacked like cakes, layer on layer, each layer different, first concrete and then cinder block and then brick (not much wood; not much work for a carpenter here)

- a juggler, with his cup, and two kids watching him, imitating him, pretending to be jugglers themselves

- a group of men trotting along in tight formation, red pants and white shirts, carrying a red and white flag, beating on sticks as the crowd made way for them

- a bank, gleaning with aluminum trim around spotless windows

- ragged men just outside that bank, intently watching two seated men playing chess or checkers

- a mule and a cart

Banners were stretched across the street. A bus was stuck at the intersection, barely able to move. The dense air here smelled of fumes, and of fried chicken; we were passing a vendor with a barbeque grill.

All in the first block.

At the end of the block that bus was in our way, but our driver bounced his motorcycle up onto the sidewalk, managed to get between the building and another soda machine, and bounced back down onto the pavement, apologizing to the pedestrians who stepped back as we pushed through.

This side street was narrower, hardly wide enough for two cars side-by-side, and dark with heavy smoky air. Did the sun ever get into these tight canyons? People were on this street, but it didn't seem to be a shopping street. The sidewalks had motorcycles and scooters, bicycles, sofas, a refrigerator, barricades, another ragged sofa, a desk with a cat sleeping underneath it, a television set, tables, file cabinets, trash bins. Alleys jogged off on both sides, twisting out of sight.

Children were running along the sidewalks with us and ahead of us. At the far end of the street, in front of a garage, amid a gang of kids, stood a very tall man, and a man, somewhat shorter, who looked like Mike. Seeing me, the man who looked like Mike sent children running toward us and toward the other end of the street.

And it was Mike. And the tall man with Mike, when we met halfway down the street, was Mr. Ruiz. Mike had told me about Enrique Ruiz, that he looked to be about twenty-five, but he was in his forties, married, with several children. He didn't tell me that Mr. Ruiz would be sporting dreadlocks and smell wonderfully of pomade. Now I was definitely not back in Taylor.

As we walked back toward the garage, I had a chance to get to know a little more about Enrique Ruiz. Dad used to have a saying, about some fellow he'd seen who was really tall and thin. He'd say that this fellow could fit inside a sipping straw and leave room for the bubbles. Now I was looking at that fellow. He was at least an inch taller than me, even without the dreadlocks and the bandanna, but I probably outweighed him by twenty or twenty-five pounds. Enormous hands. Hands that could pick a basketball up off the floor. Eyes like coals; he certainly could be a preacher, or a prophet. A scary preacher.

But he was not a basketball player. He didn't seem to understand about basketball when I asked. He and Mike got into an animated discussion. I didn't quite know what they were saying. I could catch the occasional word but couldn't put them together. They must be talking the local Creole, I realized. My friend Mike -- Silent Mike – was speaking a new language. And he'd been here three weeks.

Mike broke into my reverie. "He wants to know if you can come back and show him about basketball. Anyway, here we are."

We'd reached the garage. The second floor of the garage overhung the first, so they had a space below to work that was open but sheltered. On sawhorses under a sheet was something long and narrow. Even in December and open to the air, and with the fan running, this space was uncomfortably warm and humid.

The boys followed us in and stood wordlessly against the walls on the sides and the corrugated lift-up doors at the back. Mr. Ruiz moved to the far end of the shape on the sawhorses and said something gravely to the boys that I did not quite understand. They nodded. Then Mr. Ruiz snatched the sheet away.

There it was, what they had been working on, what the boys were eager to see: a birdcage of a dragster, but a half-sized dragster. Gleaming black tubes and tires, and a seat and an engine. Mike's dragster for kids. Out came my camera. If this didn't interest the Institute, nothing would.

"Ohhhh," came from the boys, and then an excited murmur.

"Okay," and something I didn't understand, from Mr. Ruiz.

Mike and Mr. Ruiz each grabbed a section of frame in front of the rear wheels. The boys stationed themselves around the car. I shared a handhold by one of the tiny front wheels. Mr. Ruiz shooed the boys away who were stationed on the street side of the car; that was where we were going to move the car. Then we lifted, all together.

Up went the birdcage, off the sawhorses. Lord almighty, it was heavy for a birdcage.

-- *Sawhorses yo!*

Several of the boys let go to get the sawhorses. Without them lifting, the birdcage settled right back down, fortunately without trapping any of the boys.

-- *Ezekiel. Toussaint. Sawhorses yo.* And something else, and this time two of the boys stood aside while everyone else lifted, and then, when the car was in the air, pulled the sawhorses away.

More instructions from Mr. Ruiz, as they carefully lowered the birdcage arrow until it sat, almost quivering, on the street.

That was when I realized that the street had been transformed. Barricades had appeared at each end of the street. The sidewalk was now lined with anything that was soft: mattresses, sofas, sandbags, clothes racks. People were standing and sitting everywhere.

"Wait here with the car," Mike said to me, and he and Mr. Ruiz walked up each side of the street, inspecting the barriers and moving people back. Satisfied, Mike returned.

"Ollie?" said Mike. "Where's Ollie? Where's --"

"Here I am, sir," said a small round-faced boy, tucking his shirt in as he tumbled out of the door of the garage, almost falling.

Mike looked over to me. Mr. Ruiz, at the far end of the street, lowered his head and folded his hands in prayer. I took that as a signal, but, before I could say anything, Mr. Ruiz did the blessing. Again I caught only the occasional word. Then Mike said a blessing in English; probably the same blessing. I wondered if people at the far end could hear over the nearby traffic.

Mike strapped Ollie into the seat, Ollie nodding vigorously as Mike talked and pointed. Satisfied, Mike stepped behind the cage of tubes, gripped the starter rope, and pulled. He pulled again.

At his third pull, the engine started.

Not much of a song, I thought. Sounds like a lawnmower engine. Even without a body, just bare tubing, this contraption looked so much like a genuine rail dragster that I had expected the engine to crackle like one.

The dragster began to roll forward, Mike walking with it. He'd rigged up a cable as a hand throttle. As soon as he saw that Ollie could steer in a straight line, he goosed the throttle and broke into a trot as the car spurted forward. Mr. Ruiz pointed to the crowd, then to the dragster, and clapped, and the crowd lining the street joined in.

Ollie and Mr. Ruiz got the machine stopped at the sofa barrier at the far end of the block. Ollie threw his hands in the air – the champion salute -- and climbed out. Mr. Ruiz and Mike picked up the front end and swung the dragster around. Mike was talking to people in the crowd as he went. My Mike — talking! All the way past the garage to the far end of the block, and then Mike swung it back around. The next boy climbed in, and Mike snapped the seatbelts closed.

So the next hour or so passed -- one boy after another into the driver's seat, a short slow run, a little burst of acceleration for the excitement, occasional pauses to make adjustments and once to refill the gas tank. Next!

The engine was not running well by now, and finally it quit. Mike and Mr. Ruiz exchanged glances; evidently they'd expected the engine to quit. So they waved to the crowd, which had not thinned. We rolled the racecar off the street and back into the alcove of the garage and lifted it back onto the sawhorses. Mike motioned me to follow him, and we went through the door that Ollie had burst out of.

Inside Mike turned on a fan, apologized for the air conditioner not working, and gave me a towel.

"Cold drink?"

I said no, not yet.

"Got those catalogs?"

While Mike thumbed through one of the parts catalogs I had brought, I looked at the drawings and plans pinned to the wall. Here was one of the drawings that Mike had made back at the diner in Taylor when we were still talking about the whirligig. Several penciled sketches, taken together, looked like something the birdcage on the stand had become. There was an annotated timeline, also in pencil, and several photographs, including one of a girl about the age of seven standing next to a junior dragster. The finished product. The girl was holding an enormous trophy. Her safety helmet was dangling from her wrist. She looked proud.

As I checked the gallery Mike came over and set a catalog in front of me. "This is what I want," he said, with his finger pointing to an engine. "Two of them now, if we have the money."

I looked at the price. "We can afford that."

He was also going to need money for a paint job, a good one. Enrique knew a local guy who he thought would paint the body panels cheap, but they needed a design. He already had the aluminum panels; no problem there.

"So you're staying. I meant to ask, where? Don't we have to give up the house?"

"Enrique got me a place. A real dump. Guess I'll need money for that too." While I was thinking about this development, Mike added, "Guess what? I'm learning down here. This guy can really weld. I'm learning how to weld."

"You could always weld. I've seen you."

"Not like this guy," said Mike. "Fooled you too then."

Around that time the door opened, and Mr. Ruiz stuck his head in. "All ready. Mike, Mr. Lawrence, you can come now," he said, or something close to that.

The street had been transformed again. Tables of all descriptions flooded the street: card tables, folding tables, sawhorses with boards across, large boxes. People were crowded at the tables and on the sofas and chairs. Food and drink were everywhere, and more was still arriving. The air was rich with celebration.

Mr. Ruiz led me and Mike to our waiting table in front of the garage. Our table was covered with sandwiches, a steaming hot tray, bottles, and tiny Christmas trees. I started to sit down, but Mike whispered, Not yet.

How could I forget? No one was eating yet. They were all looking to our table. Well, of course, dummy, another blessing. But no one was saying anything. Finally Mr. Ruiz gestured to me, so I did the blessing and then Mr. Ruiz repeated it, and then he called, "Come, everyone, eat." And we did.

Finally the police came on their blue and white scooters, or maybe they were soldiers. They pulled up unsmiling at both ends of the block: camo uniforms, body armor, weapons like pipes, and baby faces under their helmets. Frankly I was almost glad they came. I could not have had any more to drink or eat, and I was a little nervous about all that had been set before me and I had no idea of what it was.

The sofas blocking the ends of the street were being moved. The food was being taken away, and the tables were being folded. Mr. Ruiz hugged me and went in, and Mike said, "Well, back to work, I guess. Let's talk tonight."

Then my friend with his motorcycle was next to me. I'd forgotten all about him. I put my camera away. Before I climbed on behind him, I took a moment to look around one last time. The police were gone. Someone shook my hand.

Where was I going now? A cathedral; my friend would drop me off at the cathedral. Maybe there I could think about what I would do down here to justify myself to the Institute besides writing status reports. I told myself I was networking, building up connections that would be useful for the future. But only if they responded to my next status report. If they didn't respond to this one, I told myself, I could stop worrying about them. At least Mike was clearly achieving our mission.

A delivery van made its way down the street and stopped, blocking the way. Wires were still hanging off the poles in great bunches and leading in all directions. The cat was asleep under the desk. Again I noticed the clothes hanging from the line, two stories up, and the flowers spilling out of window boxes, the flags, the cubist walls, the intricate ironwork on the balconies and on the gratings over the windows.

Somehow I had seen something like this somewhere before. It came to me. It reminded me of pictures I had seen of the old quarters of Jerusalem. I was in Jerusalem, a new Jerusalem -- a sloppy, living, breathing place of grace.

Washed Clean

The oldest Protestant church in Central America and the oldest and largest building in New Hampton, survivor of countless hurricanes, the **Cathedral of St. Anselm** is one of New Hampton's leading sights, if only because for its green lawns and breezy location that provide a bit of a relief for the overheated traveler. The cathedral is located at the intersection of Prince Street and George Street, about a half mile south of the town center.

St. Anselm's was built by the British after their takeover of St. Guayábe in 1835 to display their newfound prestige. For five years slaves labored in its construction, using stone and brick brought over as ballast by ships coming from Europe.

Its high imposing Norman tower and fine stained glasswork have withstood countless hurricanes.

Benches around the cathedral allow visitors to enjoy the gardens and marvel at the expansive view overlooking the lower town and the Caribbean Sea.

Inside the cathedral are memorial plaques, an antique pipe organ, ornate wooden roof beams, and hand-carved pews. Formerly the cathedral also housed relics of the near-mythical St. Guayábe, but these relics were removed many years ago for safekeeping and have since been lost.

Visitors should be aware that the cathedral is currently not in service and is usually locked. To view the interior, check with your hotel desk to see if any tours or events are scheduled. Choral performances by schoolchildren for the major holidays are regularly presented and are especially enjoyable. Remember that any contributions to restore the cathedral to operation are welcomed; public donation boxes are available for this purpose.

When I was returned to the top of the hill, the cathedral was still where I had passed it an hour or two before, but it had changed. What I had seen before was "the oldest and largest building in New Hampton .. high imposing Norman tower and fine stained glasswork." This was the cathedral as the Guidebook had it.

Now I was seeing the actual cathedral, through my own eyes, and it was hardly imposing. In fact, it was dilapidated. Grass grew between the cobblestones of the plaza, and litter had blown into the crevices of the old brickwork. The flower baskets on poles like the picture in the guidebook showed were nowhere to be seen. What I did see was a construction scaffold on one corner of the plaza, to no purpose that I could discern, and a line of fluttering yellow tape a little down the hill toward Canaltown. A solitary police car sat just behind the tape.

I felt uneasy. Talk about danger; there was a danger here.

Next to the broad steps leading up to the cathedral doors was a large bulletin board. The letters read, "Closed for Renovation." At the top of the stairs a faded, curled sign announced in barely readable letters that the pageant scheduled for Easter had been cancelled. The doors were locked, of course.

I walked around to the side. The glorious stained glass was nowhere visible. Plywood sheets filled the openings.

Probably it was time to head back into town, but I did want to see the interior, with its " .. memorial plaques, an antique pipe organ, ornate wooden roof beams, and hand-carved pews." (The guidebook had also mentioned the possibility of special tours or events -- "Choral performances by schoolchildren for the major holidays are regularly presented and are especially enjoyable" – but there was no sign that any of those would be happening anytime soon.) I noticed a covered porch with double doors on the side of the cathedral. Under the porch was a dark narrow pit. Stairs led to a door at the bottom. All locked, of course.

I walked back out to the front of the cathedral, to the 'expansive square and breezy location providing a bit of relief for the overheated traveler. Benches around the cathedral allow visitors to enjoy the expansive view overlooking the lower town and the sea.' I did welcome that breeze, but the benches weren't available. One had been burned. Another was simply gone except for its massive concrete frame. But the broad steps were available, so I went over, pulled off my daypack, and sat.

Off to my left and stretching on into the afternoon haze was the sea. Along the edge of the sea were boatyards with cranes, a marina behind a breakwater. Was that where the fishing boats docked? I made a note to go down to the marina before I left; I might come back with a story. From there and reaching all the way to my right were the roofs of Canaltown, all jumbled together. One of those roofs must have been Mike's shop, but it was impossible from here to know which one.

Is there something here for Morrie? I took some pictures, realizing that this vista would just wash out on newsprint. But the tower would work, from here, so I took a few shots of that.

Just below me, across the square and hidden under the brow of the hill, were drummers keeping a steady beat. Whenever they paused, I heard rhythmic shouts that I couldn't understand. It sounded something like the cheerleading at a football game back home, but there was something darker to it.

I was wishing I'd brought a hat. The sun was intense. What must it be like in the summer?

I wanted to walk over to investigate the source of what I was hearing, but something about the sound, the police car, and the tape stopped me. Right in this spot I felt safe; moving fifteen paces toward the yellow tape did not.

What about this presentation I would be doing at Rosey's the day after tomorrow? I needed to work on that. I wasn't eager.

I confess that I have a problem with Christmas. I'm sure it's just me, but, in my preaching, I always want to talk about what Jesus should mean in our lives. Christmas is about something else. True, it is a wonderful story. All those warm, familiar songs. There's a mommy and the little baby. A long journey and then no place to stay. Cute little lambs. Shepherds. Angels in a celestial choir. Three kings led by a mysterious star. Exotic gifts. Gold! And, just to top it off, a scary bad guy who gets outsmarted. And so we have it all: a story so wonderful that we never tire of it, and tradition, and family, and that warm feeling of peace and goodness.

The problem for me is, I wish we had a story that we all know and cherish that brings us even closer to forgiving, caring, growing, accepting. What would it take to bring the Sermon on the Mount into our hearts as deeply as the Christmas story is?

Having gotten *that* off my chest, I started thinking about how to bring the story to the crowd out there at Rosey's. They're going to be party people, yacht people, well-to-do, out for a good time, but home is somewhere in the back of their minds. Let's stress the poverty of the stable and the riches of the wise men. The mommy and the little baby. Probably can say something about the shepherds and the angels who are there with hosannas of joy and praise. Let's not bring up the evil deeds of the dreadful Herod.

What I *really* wanted to do was some sort of communion celebration, maybe with some really good wine and the best bread I could find. Something to bring out the joy -- Christmas, and sharing, and community, how joy is best when everyone can share it. Share singing. Figure out a way to get people to mix. Something like I just experienced in Canaltown.

I can't assume that everyone there would be a Christian. Very well; how can I make a meal and celebration that would work for everyone? Maybe I needed to have alternative meals ready?

While I was working this all out, the police car never moved. The drumbeat was still coming from below. I decided to take a break and walk over for a closer look. What could happen?

As soon as I crossed the square and approached the tape, the police siren blared. There was no one on the upper plaza except me and the police car. I took another step and heard:

"DO NOT APPROACH THE BARRIER."

No one was near the police barrier except me. Looking over to the police car, I pointed to myself. Do you mean me?

"BACK AWAY FROM THE BARRIER."

I did as I was told and gestured, I want to go down there. Why is that a problem?

"DO NOT CONTINUE TOWARD THE BARRIER."

I guess I'm not going any farther. But why not? I went over to the police car to ask. The engine was running. The officer behind the wheel glared at me. I knocked on the window. He lowered it a crack, and I felt a wave of coolness coming from the air-conditioned interior of the car.

"Excuse me, officer, but what's going on here? What's the problem?"

The officer was thin-faced and thin-lipped, with an ironic smile on his lips. "What do you mean, what's going on here? You don't know what's going on here?"

"No, sir, I don't."

"Well, come back here Christmas day, and you'll find out." With that, he rolled his window up.

I lingered. This was as close as I had gotten to the barrier. At least from here, I could see what was down the hill. A formation was drilling down in the lower plaza, possibly the same group that had marched by Mike's garage just before lunch.

These marchers were all dressed in white pants with blue piping, white-and-blue striped pullovers, and blue bandannas. They had long black sticks or rods, batons, which they raised, twirled, thrust out, as they took a step forward, two steps to the side, a step backward, two steps to the other side, thrust the batons into the air with a loud shout, and did it all again. A line of drummers along the side of the plaza pounded out a beat.

On second glance I realized that these marchers were not the same as the group I had seen earlier near Mike's. That group was dressed in red, not blue. And the drumbeat was different from the one I had heard then. That beat had been bang-bang-BANG, bang-bang-BANG. This beat went dot-da-da-da, dot-da-da-da, dot-dot-DOT. I liked this pattern better.

And I was impressed. We used to do drill in high school. We were nothing like the group I was looking at now. They were crisp. Their timing was perfect. They moved as one. The drums never changed, never missed, never dragged. Their white and blue uniforms were spotless, perfectly in place. Did they ever tire?

And, why? What were they here to do?

After about three minutes the window of the police car was lowered. The driver said, "Why are you still here?"

"I'd still like to know what this is about. Can you help me?"

He said something, just an exclamation, as he rolled his window up.

I found my chaplain identification card and held it out for him to see. The window was opened a crack, and a hand came up to take the card. The card was passed to the hand, and the window closed.

Dot-da-da-da, dot-da-da-da, dot-dot-DOT! DA DA, dot-da-da-da, dot-da-da-da, dot-dot-DOT!

Finally the window opened, all the way this time. "You're a long way from home."

I nodded. Yes, I was a *long* way from home.

"Why didn't you say you were clergy? Come around and get in," he barked.

I circled the car. Another officer in the car, who I had not noticed before, climbed out of the front seat, and got into the back seat. He was eating a sandwich as he went.

Almost before I sat down, the officer behind the wheel said, "What are you doing here?"

What *am* I doing here? I tried the best answer I had. "I'm preparing for a Christmas service I'll be doing.

"Where's that?"

"On the beach at Pirate's Head."

"Rosey's place?"

"I believe so." I didn't know if mentioning Rosey directly was a good idea or not.

While my friend behind the wheel digested this information, his partner had never stopped eating his sandwich. I noticed that the two were wearing different uniforms. The driver was in sharply pressed whites; his partner was wearing sloppy green fatigues. I'd seen that before. Yes, at the airport. The pair at the airport that took Jack away had been dressed like that.

I took a look around the interior. In a rack behind me were black assault rifles and a grenade launcher. A large black box, vented, was bolted to the floor with wires coming out of it and binders stacked in a low box on top of it. The floor was littered with lunch wrappings.

"Will you look at those freaking gooneybirds down there. Too stupid to get out of this heat. Nothing to do but bake their brains all day long."

"And you get to sit here all day long and watch them?"

"I mean, just look how they're dressed. It's a church for chrissakes. They're outside a church. So wear something respectful, like you. Like slacks, proper shoes. A blazer. What's this with the tennies and the shorts and the tee-shirts?

"Here all day?" I repeated.

"Not us. We're only here until two. Then we leave this dump behind."

The officer in the back seat grunted his agreement through his half eaten sandwich.

"If I might ask, why do they have you here at all?"

"Orders. Somebody has to be here. But this all ends on the 26th. Just have to make three more shifts."

The other officer, the one in fatigues, said from the back seat, "Those are the *Siervos de la Madre*. My cousin is with them." The driver seemed not to hear him.

"Why does anyone have to be here?" I asked.

"You don't know? You really are a tourist, aren't you? How long have you been here?"

"I guess it's about one full day so far."

We sat in silence for some time. The driver never took his eyes off the men doing their drill in the lower plaza. The other officer never stopped eating.

I said, "How long have you been here?"

"Too long."

"You don't like it here?"

"Nothing but trouble all the time. Just little things, but the tension's driving me nuts. Listen, those gooney birds want to storm the cathedral if we weren't here. They want to take it over. You don't want to be here on Christmas. There'll be half a dozen police cars along the edge of this square. And those gooneybirds'll be over there. Shouting. Throwing stuff. They'll even have bullhorns. See that grandstand they're building? Tell you this, father, they have no sense of decency at all."

"And that's what happens, a lot of yelling and drums?"

"Yeah, and sometimes they even fight with each other, the blues and the reds. If we're lucky. But they'd take over if we let them."

"Blues and reds?"

"Blues, reds, stripes, black and green, you name it. They can't even get along with each other."

I decided not to say anything about the two different uniforms in the car. Instead, I said, "It must get a little .. uncomfortable. This has been going on for a while?"

"Every year for the last five years, ever since they closed the cathedral down."

"Longer than that," said the officer in fatigues. The driver seemed not to hear him.

"What would happen if they did get into the cathedral?" I asked the driver.

"Well, if you listen to the bleeding hearts, they just want to run some kind of a service here. 'A Christmas service, la, la'. Yeah, right! Listen, they're a bunch of savages. Some of them anyway. Drink blood. Beat drums. Sacrifice a dog. Take a dump on the dog's body. That's what they'd do. If we let them. But we won't. And that's that."

"So I can't go out there?"

"You can, if you really want to. Legally, we're only here to warn people. But if it were up to me, I'd drive 'em all out, just put an end to this nonsense. Let 'em find their own church to do their service in. Listen, I had to stop you, it was for your own good."

"Is there some way I can get into the cathedral?'

"We can't let you in. What you can do is check with your hotel or check with one of the churches in town. They must have someone who has access."

The driver turned in his seat to look me in the eye. "But listen," he said in a low voice, "And forget where you heard this, but there's the waterman. He'll be along any time now."

"The waterman?"

The driver laughed. "Get this. This is how it is around here. We have these guys working in the church, right, but there's no one in the church for five years. But every day for the past week, since we got here, okay, truck pulls up, guy gets out with a full water jug, goes in, comes out five minutes later with another full jug over his shoulder, gets in, drives away. Water for the workmen, see? Workmen who aren't there. Must be in the contract. How crazy is that?"

"They're working on the church?"

"Hey, you don't see the scaffold!"

"Yes, I did. What's it there for?"

"Who knows? Nobody there either," scoffed the policeman driver.

"And you say this 'waterman' will be around any minute now?"

"Not me," he said. "I didn't say nothin'. Maybe you better get moving. He'll be here and gone in a flash." And to his partner, he said, "Hey, d'ja save anything for me?"

I was dismissed.

Armed with my guidance, I had no trouble getting inside. I just buttoned my blazer, nodded to the delivery driver and followed him down the stairs. He ignored me. I had my identification card ready but didn't need it.

The basement was dark. Of course no lights came on when I tried the switch, but there was enough light coming from the outside door that I could see stairs leading up to the main floor. The light didn't make it to the top of the stairs. I waited in this room until the deliveryman had passed by on his way out, and then went up the stairs. In complete darkness up there, I felt around to find the knob on the door to the sanctuary, took a deep breath, opened the door – it wasn't locked – and was still in total darkness.

This had to be another small room, not the sanctuary itself. There had to be a door that opened to the sanctuary, so I crossed this room, a step at a time, until I collided with something.

It was a wall of cloth: robes hanging on a rack.

And, just to the left of the rack, was the door.

And, beyond the door was light. Not much light, but enough to see that the floor out there was clear. There was nothing out there. The Holy of Holies? A step in the right direction, anyway.

I walked out to the center of the floor. As my eyes gradually adjusted to the light, I could see that my first impression was wrong. The floor was not empty. The center of the floor was cleared, but the sides were not. Something had been pushed against the walls.

In my mind I was already writing another piece for the paper back home. But how was I going to describe this place? I didn't even remember the names of the spaces. For instance, was this place where I was standing called the 'sanctuary,' like I thought, or was the sanctuary only the raised section where the clergy celebrated the service, while the rest of the people were down here? What was a 'nave'? A 'chancel'? It had been so long since I'd been in a church that I couldn't remember. At least I knew that there was a room beyond this space, at the front end of a church. That room was called a 'narthex.' Who could forget a name like 'narthex'?

By now my eyes had adjusted somewhat, and I could see what was pushed up against the walls. There were no pews at all. Mostly there were rolled up sections of carpeting at the base of the walls. At the back, those dark shapes were doors, presumably. Over in one corner were shapes that I couldn't quite make out -- a ladder? another scaffold? a seat or a bench or maybe a sofa? something else, litter of some sort?

Mostly what I was aware of was the feel of the space. The smell of damp plaster. The humid, baking heat. The deep stillness. What a space! What an inspiring, awesome, breathtaking room. All empty, two days before Christmas. Why is that, Lord? Those people out there, the marchers and drummers, do they want to come into this space? And why can't they? This is your hall, Lord.

Why aren't the people allowed into it? Maybe a church with walls is a good thing. But an empty church is an abomination. Your birthday, and the guests are barred? What's going on here?

Maybe there was no money to run a proper church, with a minister and his assistants, a staff, musicians. But no pageant? No children's choir? No little play, with the shepherds and their lambs and their crooks, and the gloriously costumed child kings from the East? No tinsel star high above, hanging from those ornate wooden beams? So what's the problem? Money? I know from experience that putting on a pageant or a choral performance usually requires nothing much more than a willing group, some hard-working garment makers, a few phone calls, and a little publicity. A safety issue? A political issue? Maybe a sanitation issue?!

Yet the church seemed to be in good shape. The scaffolding outside, the ladder over in the corner, the water bottle delivery – someone was caring for this space. I couldn't help thinking of the house back in Taylor before we started working on it, and how much better this place smelled. I wondered if they had squirrels or other rodents. They certainly didn't have bats or birds in here.

Faint light was seeping into this cavern from around the edges of the plywood; colored light. So the stained-glass windows were still there under their protective covering? Here, I imagined, was a long story with those windows: the joy of installing the windows two centuries ago and seeing the light in all its colors plunging into the inside of the cathedral. And then the painful damage of the first hurricane, and then restoring the windows, and the second hurricane, and the third.

Something fixed me to this spot. I just wanted to stand there, not moving, seeing into the darkness, letting the quiet fill me. I thought, *Very nice. Lord, you finally get me into a church, and it's a church all for me.*

Well, that wasn't much of a prayer. The time had come to be a little more formal, so I lowered my eyes, faced front, toward where the altar would be, and prayed: *Lord, You have brought me to this Your holy home. I pray that You reveal Your will to me. Let me know Your plan for me here. Why am I in this land, oh Lord? Why am I sent here? Open my heart so that I may discern Your will. And, as always, I pray that my service be acceptable in Your sight, and fruitful to Your purpose. I ask this in His name. Amen.*

Then I looked up, into that dusty light.

The altar area was not completely empty. A high ornate pulpit towered over the worship space. What kind of a sermon would be preached from there? Certainly no sermon that I could ever preach. This was an Old Testament pulpit. From this lofty height the inspired bearer of the Word would almost be compelled to lift robed arms high to the nearby heavens to beg for a cooling rain and a gentle wind, or hurl down mighty torrents of brimstone and damnation upon the cowering congregation: *He hath unleashed His hot anger, His wrath, to make the land desolate and destroy the sinners within it.*

And there, high on the wall, was a source of light: a circular stained-glass window: a white lamb on a blue background, holding a banner that had a cross on it. So at least one piece of stained glass had survived uncovered.

I drank its light. When my thirst was satisfied, I let myself make a plan of sorts.

Before I go, it'd probably be a good idea to find the current minister or bishop, if there still is one. And then I could go around all the churches. Mr. James, we only have a week here, and we're using it up fast.

- I should find a Bible

- I should go up into that high pulpit, if only for the experience.

- I should start out for home before too long.

But for now I just wanted to let this space fill me. As I stood there, time gradually faded. The light gradually faded. Here was a hint of eternity.

Eternity with a distant but mighty rumble. The light *had* actually faded. Odd; this was still midafternoon, wasn't it? But that rumble was real. Something was happening outside. I wondered if this was the midafternoon shower that I'd read about in the guidebook: '.. often a shower, sometimes heavy, around three p.m.' It certainly sounded like rain on the roof. Heavy rain.

I went toward the back of the cathedral and into the narthex. Through one of the small windows in the high, arching doors, I could see a blur but nothing more, so I slipped a door open just a crack.

Coming down in the square was a solid mass of water. This was a deluge like nothing I'd ever seen. Five seconds of this would drench a person. I could barely see the police car. From across the street, I thought I could hear faint but steady chanting. Those people – the marchers, the protesters, whoever they were – hadn't left. They meant it.

Cooler air was coming in, so I propped the door slightly open, found a folding chair, and stayed. Clearly no one could see me. Just as obviously, I wasn't going anywhere anytime soon.

I wanted to go out into it, get myself drenched: *Let us draw near to God with a sincere heart and with the full assurance that faith brings, having our hearts sprinkled to cleanse us from a guilty conscience and having our bodies washed with pure water.* But I was afraid I'd be seen, so I just waited by the door, for I don't know how long.

Finally the rain stopped. It didn't slacken, it just stopped. One minute it was pouring; the next, a few drops were still falling, the drops that didn't see the memo and thought they were supposed to be only a gentle shower, and the sun was already coming out. Judging from the hammering and sawing from across the street, the crew over there had gone back to work on their grandstand. The police tape was drooping; rainwater was dripping from it. The drums began pounding louder.

I listened. I've heard drums like that before. Yes I have: Carolyn and I back at the Variety Theatre, watching a jungle epic with the drums, wondering what the drums were saying; Carolyn wide-eyed, holding my arm tight with one hand and mechanically eating her popcorn with the other.

Then I pushed the outside cathedral door all the way shut. No reason to take a chance of getting caught. With the door closed, the drums were fainter.

I looked around the narthex. Covering one wall were children's crayon drawings. One had fallen on the floor. On another wall was a plaque with a list with the names of all the bishops. Another plaque commemorated the coronations of four native kings of the Ixtani tribe 'in ceremonies that rivalled the great ceremonies of European royalty.' Still another plaque gave the history of the church, as reported in the guidebook, except that the cathedral it was modeled after was now in West Sussex instead of East Sussex. On a chalkboard was a list of 'this year's pledges,' including the amounts. A flyer on an iron stand advertised a 'genuine olde worlde British breakfast, complete with all the trimmings' for £3.50, or $6.00 American. The menu made me wish I was hungry, but the date told me I was about five years too late.

Over there was a chest of drawers, with a rack of pamphlets: How to Save Your Marriage. What to Say to Your Teenager. Having Trouble Sleeping? What You Need to Know About Bequests. Tending Your Heavenly Garden. The pamphlets were all curled and drooped over. I was looking for a Bible but didn't find one. I did find a flashlight in a drawer of the chest, but the batteries were dead.

I knew I had to be going, but I wasn't ready to leave.

Come to the Table

Back in the sanctuary the light had returned, somewhat, but it was getting darker fast. Avoiding the pulpit for now, I did a little more exploring. In an alcove at the side of the church – a nave? a transept? – was a rack of votive candles in glass jars. I picked up one of the glass jars and lit the candle for Carolyn.

On the shelf below the candles was a Bible. Now all I needed was a place to sit while I found a few passages to read. I remembered the seat or bench or sofa in the corner where the workmen were repairing the wall. Taking a candle, that's where I went.

What the workmen had was a seat from a car. The workmen had set their corner up nicely. In addition to the seat and the ladder, they had their tools and buckets, a small icebox, a generator, a large fan, a tape deck / radio, and the top-loading water dispenser. A newspaper on the floor had a November date, so they'd been here recently. I decided not to check the icebox.

I went back to get more candles. Setting them on the steps of the ladder, I lit them for light, and settled down on the car seat. Holding the Bible, I just breathed. There was something actually comforting about the wet plaster smell, or maybe it was just good to hold a Bible again. I went back to a thought I'd had before, which was, Maybe I'm supposed to be here just to be here. Maybe I'm not here to do something. Maybe I'm here to heal. Like a cat. Like a cat of mine once who'd been a little sick and then disappeared one day. Months later I found what was left of her under the porch. She'd crawled to a safe and quiet space. And that's where it ended for her. Sometimes cats make it back, and sometimes they don't. Just wait to find out which it's going to be.

I put the Bible down. I really had to catch up on my reading, but I wasn't about to hurry just yet. Well, I could just mosey up toward the pulpit. By the way, there's an organ up there. I'd always wanted to play the organ. Probably not a good idea now, though. Police car outside and all. While we're not doing that, probably a good idea not to try to start the generator either.

Jonah had been on my mind ever since the plane ride and even before. Let's see what Jonah has to say. Jonah, who spent three days in the belly of a great fish. Jonah, who tried to run away from God. And then, when the fish threw him out on the beach ('spewed him out', in fact), he did do what God wanted of him: He went to the great wicked city to tell them to repent.

And they did!

How would that story be told today? Flying in, there I was, in the belly of this great bird, on my way to a great city – great at least compared to Taylor. When I landed, Jack and Mike would be there to greet me, and I would cry out, Repent! Repent! And they would be embarrassed mightily. Which is sort of how it went, except I never got a word out and we were all dumped into the cauldron with police and the girl in tears and litter on the floor.

I went to open the Bible, but, before I could find Jonah, I remembered another Biblical fish. It was where? It was .. it was in a dream of Peter's -- a blanket, and a fish, all kinds of creatures.

I found the passage and read, in the wavering light:

… he fell into a trance, and saw heaven opened, and a certain vessel descending upon him, as it had been a great sheet knit at the four corners and let down to the earth: Wherein were all manner of four-footed beasts of the earth, and wild beasts, and creeping things, and fowls of the air. And there came a voice to him, Rise, Peter; kill, and eat.

But Peter said, Not so, Lord; for I have never eaten any thing that is common or unclean.

And the voice spake unto him again the second time, What God hath cleansed, that call not thou common. This was done thrice: and the vessel was received up again into heaven.

So there were no fish on the blanket after all, but that wasn't what struck me; I'm wrong just about as often as I'm right. What did strike me was that Jonah and Peter had roughly the same story: unexpectedly called away from their lives to deliver an unwelcome message from God.

Peter was puzzled by his dream, the Bible tells us, and so was I. So I

made myself comfortable on the seat,
held the book,
closed my eyes,
and thought about what I had read, and thought
That's when I heard the voice.

A voice? Was someone here? And then a thump. Something had struck my foot. What was it? What's going on here? Have I been discovered? Am I in trouble now?

I looked down. It was the Bible. I'd dropped the Bible on my foot.

Now I was alert again. No one was there and no voice. I was alone and it was quiet.

I knew it was time to leave this place. There couldn't be all that much more daylight outside. Between that meal I'd had at lunch, and the lack of sleep from the night before, I wasn't going to last much longer. I told myself I'd find just one more passage to read. I was going to go to Jonah now, so I picked up the Bible and rested for just a moment before opening it.

There was that voice again, holding a high, clear musical note. Gripping the Bible tightly, I shook myself and made myself continue. Now I was looking for Paul. My other rock and sustainer, and comforter always. He was forever writing to his brothers and sisters. His brothers and sisters. My brothers and sisters. How about my actual brother and sister? No problem there, none for me, thanks. What would that have been like? But there's Carolyn; she was as close as any sister could be. Should I have done more for her, tried harder? I was always too passive with her. Or maybe I did the best I could, nobody's perfect. And Erin? Thank the Lord for Mrs. Beswick, because I certainly could not have raised her by myself. and Erin's all I could have wanted her to be.

I thought of my brothers and sisters at the beach, on Christmas at Rosey's and how was I going to find bread and wine for them? Did they even have bread here? I hadn't seen any, but then, I really hadn't seen anything here yet. I'd been here hardly more than a day. What about wine? How about rum? Rum is fun. But wine is fine.

That's when I started transitioning.

I don't remember exactly how it went, but the sequence was something like this: Wine. Wine would be nice. This is all nice. I can think about wine for a while. My hurry can wait. This won't take any time. It's so nice to be in the cathedral. Filled with wine and the Spirit. No, that's not it. Is that it? But it's nice.

So I let the candlelight flow into me like warmed honey, and thought about 'nice,' and 'ice' and 'rice.' What else? Well, there's 'splice,' which doesn't quite fit in, and 'thrice,' which is the Trinity, and 'flice,' which is not a word, and a lot of other combinations of letters until I finally came up with 'slice' and got frustrated with myself because I knew there had to be more rhymes, but I was just too lazy to come up with them. They were shimmering just out of reach, but I didn't have the energy to stretch out and grasp them.

Actually, by now there were more. More what? Something more was shimmering. By now I was standing, not sitting, with my back to the wall of the cathedral. And now there was not one voice but several, coming from below me. A children's choir.

Below me? So? They had to be coming from somewhere, why not below. I decided to listen to the voices, for just a little while. They were nice.

Nice, but odd. The voices were so clear, yet I couldn't make out a word of what they were singing. They sounded celestial. Also odd was the light. The stained-glass window above the altar was now a black disc, yet the immensity of the space in front of me was filled with a hazy glow. Where could that light be coming from?

Does it matter?

Maybe, I could forget 'nice,' try another word. But I still had to get moving. I couldn't just stay here forever. Finally, with an effort, I stood up, not remembering that I had already been standing.

No matter. At least all of me was standing now, as far as I could tell. Pushing myself forward, I ventured over to the edge of the loft. I was in a loft now. There was no choir down there. All I saw at first was seething motion, and it was coming closer. No, it was me; I and the loft were slowly descending toward the floor.

As I descended, I could see more clearly.

Everything and everyone was there, and they were all singing – the children in white robes, our marchers from outside, the policemen in their several uniforms, the cabbies, the businessmen, the old man with the balloons. A long chanting procession weaved through the throng, carrying banners and a pallet. On the pallet was an open casket, and the corpse in it was sitting up, singing.

Up front were tables in the altar area, a banquet, and the men in their suits at the tables were bursting forth in song. The altar area was filled with balloons. When the procession came to the altar area, the singing corpse and its casket were gone. Now on the pallet was a bride, adorned with jewels for her husband.

Then I looked and saw again, not a bride but a creche, with a babe. We're here for the Child. Is there any greater miracle than a newborn child? Holding her in my hand, I was. And, from the other direction, a conga line, swinging smoky censers that trailed clouds of stinging incense.

I heard drumming, discordant, and a distant shout that became a mariachi band, with the guitarists wearing Santa hats. Even the dragster I'd seen that morning was there, singing. Everyone on the street that had come out to watch was there too.

Liveried waiters were going through the crowd with platters of hors d'oeuvres: Peter and Paul hauled platters aloft. Do not spurn what I have put before you.

I heard a voice from the altar area. It was our lady from next door. In song she was inviting me down for a spot of tea. I knew Hal and Morrie and Mac, Sarah and Vickie, Mrs. Beswick, and all the rest of them were down there too – I just knew it, somehow – but I wasn't ready to find them yet. Seven enormous dark-skinned men passed near me, stepping over the workmen's tools. They were playing ukuleles and singing:

All the people around from here
They come to sing from far and near
It's this starry babe they seek
This Wonder child so mild and meek.

By now I was just above the floor. What a crowd! People of all sizes and colors, dressed in every kind of clothes. Some of them were soaked, dripping from the rain, but what I noticed most were the hats – sombreros and cowboy hats, homburgs and bowlers, military helmets and crash helmets and football helmets, tweed caps and baseball caps, panama hats and berets, Sou'westers, shawls and scarves and veils, flowers and feathers, fedoras and pork pies, little pillboxes, a floppy straw hat. I knew that hat – that was the hat my frightened friend from the airport was wearing. Of course she was here too. Frightened eyes.

All around the floor were tables of every description: card tables, folding tables, improvised tables made up from sawhorses with boards, large boxes. Everywhere was a feast: food and drink, sandwiches, steaming hot trays, bottles, and tiny Christmas trees.

This is wonderful, I thought. But something is not quite right. They should all be sitting together at one table, not scattered at separate tables. Then I saw that I was mistaken; they *were* all sitting at one long table, all mingling: police, marchers, the bishop, my motorcycle driver, even the cabbie who wouldn't bring me here. And they all were calling me to come join them. They were lifting and lowering Christmas candles in unison, piercing the darkness. The tables were heavy with food.

They were singing,

Come to the table, come to the feast, come with us, come.

And then the candles faded, the light faded, it all faded, all but that sound: 'Come.'

The sound hung in the darkness, low and steady, almost not there.

I've read somewhere that there is a base sound vibrating in the universe, a low hum that lingers when every other sound has disappeared. Was that the sound I was hearing? 'Come.' Say it. 'Come.'

Then I was swimming, floating to the top of the cathedral, rising up to the heavens. It was cooler up here, and the sky was dark.

Stars flickered like candles.

Candles were flickering like stars.

Where was I? Wherever it was, it wasn't where I had just been.

I was awake?

I was lying on a sofa. I sat up. No, it wasn't a sofa, it was a car seat. I was in a cathedral, in New Hampton, St. Guayábe. And I needed to get up.

The hum had faded. The feeling that I needed to get up, and soon, was not fading. I didn't want to leave this spot and this dream, but I had no choice.

Beyond the faint light from the votive candles I'd brought over was absolute darkness. I had to go downstairs, and I couldn't see a thing.

I needed to go but I wasn't ready yet. I wanted to hold the dream for as long as I could. I asked, Is this what you want of me, Lord? This room filled? Praising you all together? Maybe not; if I was really serious, I would not be 'asking,' I would be begging. But the feeling didn't go away. Maybe this was the best I could do right now. I had to hope that it all – the dream, the feeling -- didn't totally disappear on me when I finally did move.

My body couldn't wait any longer. I took one of the candles from the ladder and plunged into the darkness. As I went, I held the light tightly, lightly. It was hot.

This. Do this.

Birds of the Air

That next morning, when I left the cathedral, I wasn't quite sure who I was. Like Peter, I was puzzled, perplexed, wondering. Deeply troubled would be more like it. I was wondering what I was supposed to do now. I frankly wasn't even quite sure who I was. But at least I was in better shape today than yesterday and the various cards in my wallet could establish my legal identity, and I decided to settle for that for the moment.

At the front of the cathedral were now two police cars in the faint light, engines faintly growling. Across the way but out of sight came faint chanting. Some things don't change, I thought.

I turned back toward town and home. There parked in the street behind the cathedral was a familiar van – Jack's Lawn Service. Well, of course. This morning has them waiting for me. Why wouldn't there be another night in the van, someone waiting for someone else here in St. Guayábe? Happens all the time.

They were asleep. Jack was slumped over the steering wheel. Mike was sprawled against the door on the other side. I wondered if Mike's friend was stretched out in the back but couldn't see. I knew I should wake them up, but didn't have the heart to, so I went back to the side porch of the cathedral to sit on the steps and write up my dream until they woke up on their own.

When I'd finished my notes, they were still asleep. I didn't need more sleep ar this point; I'd caught up on my lost sleep in the cathedral. They did; they'd been up all night looking for me. So I walked around the cathedral, trying to find the bishop's manse or a church office, without success.

They still weren't awake, so I strolled across the boulevard to visit the old cemetery, where the tombstones did indeed

".. bring back memories of the bishops and governors, businessmen and generals, native chiefs and humble sailors, the Englishmen and their wives and children, who over the course of time succumbed to the many dangers of this fetid shore.'

Back at the steps I reviewed my notes for the Christmas service and added a few thoughts. For a moment the memory of my frightened friend at the airport flashed in my mind. What was I going to do about that, if anything? Try the police station?

Something was telling me that going there was not a good idea, but it would kill some more time.

By now I had a plan. My slumbering companions could get their rest while I strolled up to the town square, counted to ten, or maybe twenty, and then head back. I wrote up a note, left it under the windshield wiper of the van, and headed toward the town center.

But then I digressed. My confusing life here just seemed to have a life of its own. Instead of counting, I made a quick stop at the police station, to reassure myself regarding my little friend. There, when I introduced myself, the first thing the officer at the desk told me was, yes, we do have a Missing Person report on you. He called for a sergeant. When the sergeant came, he verified my identity and had me sign some papers.

What about my friend from the airport? I thought that her first name was Amanda.

The sergeant and the desk officer exchanged glances. Then the desk officer, without any review, said that they had no record of such a person. He asked if I had checked with the local hospital. That would be the modern building around the corner on the Square.

The sergeant came around the desk, led me through the lobby and out onto the porch with the pillars. Pointing to the far end of the Square, he said, 'There it is, Phipps Memorial; you might try down there.'

I thanked him and set forth in the direction he had indicated. I was sure he was watching me as I went. I knew I should have gone back down the hill, which was my plan, but I didn't want to risk it with him watching me, if he was. And, besides, I was on a quest now, and the van would probably gone by then anyway.

As I went, I was puzzled by one thought. I may not know all that much about the police here yet, but they had to know about my new friend. After all, they'd picked her up at the airport. But, by what they said, they knew nothing. What was all that about?

Phipps Memorial was quiet and almost empty once I'd gotten past the lobby security. Through an opening in a thick glass pane, the receptionist apologetically told me that I would have to wait a bit. They were having trouble with their new computing system. She asked if I knew anything about computers. I had to tell her I didn't. I wasn't going to tell her that all I knew about computers was what I'd learned from science fiction movies. Did she know that her computer might go berserk and try to take over the hospital on its way to taking over the whole world? I was never going to go near any computer, Are you safe back there?

But the receptionist looked safe enough, so far, and fortunately the reception area was especially calming -- blue indirect lighting, leather chairs, an aquarium, soft music, and a distant hum that was maybe air conditioning or maybe not.

Three other people were in the waiting room: a couple, of indeterminate age, and a young person, in her late teens or early twenties. It was hard to know why or how long they were there. I guessed that the sunburn cases came in later.

I studied the couple. She wore a frilly top, trimmed in yellow, and a white swirly skirt. He had on sandals, striped multicolored Bermuda shorts, and a polo shirt with some sort of emblem on the right breast. They were both reading paperback books and did not look up.

While I was studying them, the young person came over and sat next to me. She had a story. She needed money. But she wasn't begging. She had something she could sell me. Have I tried the weed down here, she asked. It's only $5 a kilo, which is a great deal when you think that this stuff would cost $20 easy back in the States. And the best part is that it's amazing stuff, dynamite weed, it'll take you all the way there.

"Uhh," I said, working on my answer, which was that back home we only dynamite weed when all else had failed. Before I could finish forming up the words, the receptionist signaled me to come over. The receptionist regarded my young entrepreneur with some disdain, dismissed an aide or nurse that had come into her reception area, then handed me a page of printed directions to the Municipal Health Authority. I might want to check over there.

When I entered the Municipal Health Authority building, just off the Square, it was as if I had returned to Canaltown: the same pulsing street scene, the same crying babies and giddy girls, people asleep on benches, raised voices here, people huddled together there.

I joined the line that started at the doors and stretched all the way across the room. Off at the far wall was the receptionist's desk. It was right out on the floor, surrounded by a tape barrier. A policeman – this one in camo -- stood alert next to the desk. One by one the people approached the desk. No one here was wearing frilly tops with yellow trim or polo shirts with an emblem on the right breast, and they did not all look or talk the same. The line moved slowly. It seemed each person arriving at the desk had a story.

I was watching the policeman at the desk. He was having a wordless conversation with someone near me. Then the policeman signaled to someone in my direction. Getting no response, he signaled again. It dawned on me that he might be signaling me. He was. Yes, you. Step forward.

Was I going to lose my place in line? But he clearly meant me. I went forward. The people in front of me silently made way for me.

The receptionist, who had not looked up at all before, looked up at me wordlessly, impatiently. Was she annoyed?

I told my story quickly. Her first name might be Amanda. Not a medical emergency. Dressed .. well, like a hippie -- beads and scarves, purple,. Frilly hat. Sorry I don't know more. (I was starting to feel foolish – what chance did they have of finding anybody in this place, let alone someone from as little information as I had.) Frankly I couldn't remember clearly – some reporter I am! When I said that this person Amanda had probably come in sometime yesterday, the receptionist held up a hand to stop me. English? the receptionist asked, and, when I said, Well, American, she picked up an intercom microphone and started to speak into it. Nothing happened. The microphone was dead. She put it down with a look of disgust.

-- Wait over there please.

-- You can help me?

-- Wait over there please. Next person.

Out on the floor all the benches were occupied, but a heavy-set woman – Indian? -- moved herself and her children off a bench to offer me her space. That's not right, I thought, but she insisted, as did the bystanders. I was going to sit whether I wanted to or not. At least I could help entertain her children, so I did, with some finger tricks I'd learned along the way.

By now, the line went past the double doors and along the back wall.

I was running out of finger tricks when I was nudged. Alerted, I looked up. People were pointing to the receptionist's desk. The receptionist was waiting for me impatiently. Standing next to her was a large man who regarded me with interest.

The receptionist spoke briefly to the enormous man, who laughed. He had a terrible laugh – haw! haw! – like a crow. Then she pointed me out to him, and he came across the floor to me. He was so large that his hands and feet could not move in their normal arcs, but had to swing around his bulk. He wasn't walking, he was swimming. That was it; he looked like a sea creature, a seal or a walrus. A walrus, yes, with his curling moustaches, tiny eyes, and round, overstuffed face.

"Mr. Archer Hindman-Pryce at your service. My card, sir."

Time to get 'er done, Mr. James. Best behavior please. I briefly glanced at his card and found one of mine.

"A deacon, sir?" he said, squinting at my card. "You are a chaplain?" I nodded. "Very interesting, sir. We do see clergy in here from time to time. Now, please, how may I be of assistance to you?"

I explained my mission.

He listened, almost absently it seemed. "I believe I see. May I ask you a question?" Seeing no objection, he continued. "You see, sir, you haven't given us much to go on. I must say, even if you had, our records will almost undoubtedly say nothing about this person. It may only be that the paperwork is not complete. Or it may be that she is truly not here. As one gentleman to another, I hope I don't need to explain further. May I have your word on this?"

I had no idea what he was talking about but saying so didn't seem like a good start. "I'm sorry. I didn't mean to take your time."

"That's perfectly all right. I am at your service. Now, if you'll please step this way."

I was baffled. I wasn't getting this at all. My word regarding what? Still not having any idea, I simply followed him.

We went through a door and into a hallway. A faint acid smell hung in the air.

"Now that we're away from that ..," he couldn't find the word, "perhaps I can hear you better. Please do go over your problem again."

I repeated what I had said outside in the main reception room. He drew steadily on his pipe as I went over the whole story, how I had encountered her at the airport and comforted her, how I had gathered up her belongings and her purse. I told him who I was and what had brought me here.

"Ah, so you were one of the gentlemen at the airport? I believe I *can* help you. Please do follow me." He started down the hall, and I followed. "And you are from America? What does a deacon do there?" And then he stopped. He pulled out the card I had given him. "I believe I've just seen your name. Now why would that be?" Before I could say anything, he answered his own question. "Yes .. yes .. it seems you may have been missing. Are you, or have you been found?"

"It's another long story," I began. Basically I told him I had been cleared by the police authorities.

"Of course. Our wretched reporting system .. Let's see how long it takes for us here to find out you're not missing. In the meantime …"

We passed from one corridor to another. Every bench was full: people sleeping, blankets, food hampers, babies. At every nurses' station my guide had a few smiling words with the nurses -- "haw! haw!" I noticed that these stations had people huddled in the corners, wearing street clothes, seemingly with no reason to be there. When we passed the occasional lounge, the smell emerging from the door was humanity itself: urine, sweat, funk, food. The smell of Canaltown -- Canaltown North.

He had drawn my story out of me, my local address, my friends, my contact information, my experience of St. Guayábe so far. Now I learned his, so far as the hospital was concerned.

He was assuring me that much work had gone into improving their registration procedure and system. Of course, any problems that were brought to his attention were addressed immediately. Still, it did happen, as I may have been aware from certain rumours, or soon would be, that from time to time there were people in the hospital who were not registered. Sadly, some of these rumours had circulated widely, even appearing in the newspapers. According to these stories, these were former patients who had been discharged but did not leave, family members of the staff who were being tucked into various corners in order to enjoy free food and shelter, even people who just came off the street.

These stories were not only quite exaggerated but also pernicious, because they undercut the image of the hospital and caused the community to lose faith in the hospital's administration and focus. Much valuable time had to be diverted into assuring all responsible parties that the greatest diligence was devoted to the prevention of any possible incursions.

True, he had to acknowledge, despite his best efforts and those of his staff, the occasional abuse did occur. One of his very important functions was to root out any such instances, to ensure that the resources of the hospital were truly dedicated only to those in need of them.

We turned the corner into another corridor, stepping over people resting or sleeping on the floor.

That having been said, he went on, it was true that the hospital experienced ongoing problems. Despite intense efforts to secure the necessary funding, security and maintenance issues did persist. The door we had first come through, for instance, had a secure code, but the code didn't work, which was why the door catch had been taped open. This bathroom here, like so many here, is no longer functional. The internal communications system functions only intermittently. Perhaps if more people could be made aware of these deficiencies, of which I had seen only a small sample, the resulting clamour might lead to much-needed corrective action.

We had stopped at a double door. The words "STAFF ONLY BEYOND THIS POINT" were written across the doors. Mr. Hindman-Pryce pressed numbers on the security pad. Nothing happened. He dug for a key.

With the "STAFF ONLY BEYOND THIS POINT" double door behind us, the corridor was empty and quiet, although just as shabby. Paint was peeling off the walls, but the floor was swept clean. A single naked lightbulb hung from the ceiling. Halfway down the corridor, he stopped by a narrow staircase on our left – almost too narrow for him, I thought. Taking a deep breath, he pushed himself into the tight slot and started climbing. I followed, as always.

At the top of the stairs we entered a new world. It was a long and narrow room, a day room, perhaps 40 feet by 20 feet, with a long row of windows in rusting frames along one wall that looked over the rooftops to a wonderfully expansive view to the east: the harbor, the offshore islands, the distant clouds.

True, it was still shabby, but care had been taken with it – the pictures on the wall, curtains on the long row of windows, a rug, no broken furniture. The room wasn't crowded or littered, and it didn't smell of humanity. At the far end of the room were nurses in starchy white uniforms eating their lunches.

As we entered, a woman, not dressed as a nurse, was standing and talking in a high, sing-song voice.

She was as I had seen her at the airport two days ago: stretch pants, strings of beads and a purple shawl, a light, lacy blouse over a corset bodice.

She was very pale, oval faced, with unkempt blonde hair, more or less straight on one side and curly on the other, as if she had had to leave halfway through an appointment with her hairdresser.

"Oh, dear," the woman cried, pointing toward us as we entered. "Look who just came in. That dear walrus again. And a goose? A walrus and a goose!"

I had found Amanda.

"But listen," she cried out to the nurses as she stepped away from the table. "People may laugh, but the walrus is a remarkable creature. In fact, scientific surveys have shown that the walrus is the sixth most popular species in the world, behind only the panda, the chimpanzee, the lion, the monarch butterfly, the sea turtle, the elephant, the giraffe, and the great snowy owl. And do you know why? Because the walrus is so cute and loveable. Have any of you ever seen a walrus?"

The nurses giggled. One, to hide her reaction, raised her hand and said, "I saw a walrus once. In the zoo. When I was in San Diego, in California."

"That's right," answered our lady in purple. "And they're all along the shores of the Pacific. And the San Diego Zoo is a wonderful zoo. Has anyone else been there? You must go if you ever have the chance.

"And they have walruses there. Now the walrus, they live for at least fifty years, and they mate for life. Of course they mate for life. Who couldn't love a face like this?" And she puffed up her face until it was round and her eyes were tiny. Mr. Hindman-Pryce smiled indulgently.

"And the walrus walks like this." She wasn't the least bit embarrassed as she lurched around the small space in front of the tables, somehow becoming almost tall and enormous. Her hands and feet were swinging in an arc around her suddenly large bulk. The group was delighted. "That is, of course, especially if walruses could walk. Which of course they can't." The nurses tried to hide their giggles. Mr. Hindman-Pryce nodded, still smiling.

"Oh, but they're not funny. Of course they look funny but, really, they're loving, and they sing. But they don't walk. I wish I could get down on the floor to show you how the walrus actually gets around, but my clothes are clean today, thank you very much,' she waved to one of the nurses. "So let's talk about the daily life of the walrus," and she talked about the diet of the walrus family, and their grooming behavior, and how they raised their young. I confess that my knowledge of walrus life is limited, so I didn't know if she was or wasn't making up her facts as she went along.

"So that is my story of the walrus for today," she was concluding. "Just one of the many fascinating stories from nature's wonderful world. Thank you again so very much," she finished, and waited for our reaction. I clapped. The nurses were shaking with the giggles as they pretended to go back to their lunches.

Mr. Hindman-Pryce whispered to me, "Do you want to talk with her for a few moments?'

"Should I? She seems safe enough here," I whispered back. A look of consternation flashed across his face. "Wait, yes, I do," I said. "I've come this far, I guess."

"Of course. I shall await you at that small table by the far window." He waddled away, his arms swinging around him. The nurses were finishing their lunches quickly. A giggle came from the direction of the table.

I found a place next to her. "Excuse me. Are you Miss Amanda from Rosey's? May I talk to you for a moment?"

She appeared puzzled, but, before I could remind her that we'd met before, she said, "You don't look like a goose when you're sitting down, do you? Do you know the life of the goose? Actually there are many different kinds of geese. To start with, there's the .. "

"I hate to interrupt but I have only a few minutes." I had all afternooon, actually, but Mr. Hindman-Pryce-Jones probably didn't. "I just wanted to make sure you were all right."

"Of course I'm all right. Why wouldn't I be. It's very nice here."

Did she even remember me from yesterday? It *was* yesterday, wasn't it? No, it was the day before.

"Actually I'm not supposed to leave here, you know. I'm not even supposed to leave this room. Of course sometimes I have to. But they have to sneak me out. They don't allow chamber pots in here. They say some of the other lounges are really awful. Smelly and dirty. But I haven't been there. I haven't been anywhere but here since they brought me here. I don't even know how long I've been here, I think a couple of days or maybe a week. It's really very nice here, especially at lunchtime, but then it gets lonely when they all have to go back to work. But it's still better than sleeping on a bench in the square. Especially when it rains. But I used to camp in the woods by the beach, and I had a tent, a very nice one. I liked it there."

"So it sounds like you're doing very well here." I couldn't think of anyhing else to say.

She was going right on. "It's good here. It's not wonderful but it's good. It's better than jail. Actually it's about like jail here, except for this view. Isn't this view wonderful? But actually jail isn't so bad, not like they say. I've been in jail sometimes too. I was in jail last week, I think."

The nurses had left, had returned to their shifts.

She stopped, looked at me closely. "Wait. Do I know you? You were that nice man at the airport? You had a Bible, a little one?"

Amanda wanted me to know that she knew all along I wasn't really a goose, but she had to say it, she just couldn't help herself, and she hoped I didn't mind because she would never want to offend me because I must be a man of the cloth and she had always wondered what was it like to be so specially singled out by God and did I have a personal relationship with God like He would sometimes speak to me even though that was crazy to hear voices but not if it was the voice of God because she really did believe in God even though she didn't think it was necessary to go to church because God is all around us and He is love and if you loved someone you wouldn't push them away all the time but you would let them just be themselves and hold them and hug them and let them be your special friend except God can't hug because

God is a spirit and maybe being hugged by a spirit might not be so much fun after all.

She hesitated, then plunged in again. "Of course I love the bible, but sometimes people do funny things with it and use it to condemn people. Not that there's anything really wrong with bible thumpers because there really is a lot of wisdom in the bible and I've always said that if a person really follows the bible that they'd almost have to be a better person than people who don't read the bible because the bible is really all about God and love and caring and there's nothing wrong with that at all, is there?"

She hoped I didn't mind if she could just ask me one simple question and I could answer it any way I wanted because it was all right with her no matter what I said. "So, is it true that God forgives all sins? Really? But my mother always said that God will forgive us if we just come in prayer and ask and pray."

She was unleashed. "Because I know I've sinned. Forgive me father, for I have sinned. But not really, just against myself. I've always prayed that He would tie me to the rock, just not yet, because I want to be human first, and that's what being human is all about, that and forgiveness when you've been human maybe a little too much. Father, I think that deep down I'm a good person, no matter what they say. I'm not who they say I am. So I've had fun, and sometimes people give me presents, and that's very nice of them, but I'm not that kind of girl, I only take the presents because their feelings would be hurt if I didn't or when I really needed them. You must hear these stories a lot. Where are you from? I'm from Lake Claire. That's in Atlanta, in Georgia. Have you ever heard of it? It's so nice there, except that the people are so nice which makes it so hard to talk to them, but I miss it, but on the other hand I don't miss it now, because the snow is coming if it hasn't already started and is there snow where you come from but it can be hard to get the weather from back home, but who needs it, because the snow, I mean, it's really a hardship and a lot of work and you could get sick which is really why I like being down here in St. Guayábe, where it's so warm and the people are so friendly, so what's going to happen here is that I think they'll let me stay .."

She was a torrent now.

" … I think they'll let me stay because I try to help every way I can, and I can do errands, I help, make tea and coffee, cleaning up, so they say they're going to get me a nurse's uniform and then

I'll be like an assistant nurse, but what I really want to do is go back to the beach except sometimes when I sleep on the beach which is sometimes all the mosquitoes which is why I have these red blotches on my face but now they're going away and I really shouldn't even point them out because my mother told me when I was a little girl that all the boys would notice whatever you said about yourself so it was a good idea to always present your best side because that was what people really wanted to see anyway because if you smile the whole world smiles with you but if you cry all you get is a wet handkerchief and I hope that no one is upset with me because when I was at the airport I think and I wasn't really crying… "

I glanced over to Mr. Hindman-Pryce at the far table. This conversation was rapidly getting out of control, and I was ready to be interrupted. After all, it wasn't like this was some drunken angry biker at a bar back home where I seemed to know exactly what to do and had the patience to do it.

" … and I wasn't really crying because I just thought I saw a friend but it seemed like he didn't want to see me but that was all right because it happens to me all the time now even though I don't know why because I'm really a nice person but sometimes that's the way it goes and all you can do is smile and be happy and hope that the world smiles with you because it's all going to come out all right in the end like my mother said if you can just keep a song on your lips and a prayer in your heart so that was what I always try to do even if it isn't always easy and sometimes you just feel like you're filling up with tears and drowning in your tears and you might even burst from all the tears filling every part of you inside but if you thought like that it might come true and you don't want that, do you, so I just keep smiling and – excuse me?"

Mr. Hindman-Pryce was looming above us. "Please pardon my interruption," he said to her directly, "but our friend really needs to be going soon, I'm sure, so," to me, "if you've been able to attend to your question, I also should really be getting back along to my office."

"Amanda, it looks like I'll have to go now. I hope you understand." An impulse came over me. "May I give you my blessing?'

She obediently bowed her head. She looked suddenly frightened. I prayed, *"Dear Lord, in a world of stress, bring us Your peace.*

In a world of pain, bring us Your comfort. In a world of fear, bring Your love to us, Your children, and carry us in your strong hand until we can be with You, safely under Your soft wing forever. Amen."

The instant I got the words out, Mr. Hindman-Pryce took me by the arm and gently guided me toward the door. I was thinking about my prayer. Strong hand? Soft wing? Too confusing; I could do better.

But again, her suddenly frightened look.

At the door back out to the main waiting room, Mr. Hindman-Pryce said, "I do hope you have enjoyed your review of our facility. Please do not forget our need. Even a word in the right place or the smallest helping hand will be of service. And now, my good sir, it has been my pleasure," and he opened the door for me into the main waiting room.

The Blind Leading the Blind

That evening Jack and I finally found ourselves at the house together and awake. Mike hadn't come in yet. Jack was relaxing, with his feet up on a hassock, and he was declaiming. "I really admire you. You are truly something else. You disappear for a whole day and a half, come back with a story about how you were locked up in a cathedral the whole night, and we all believe every word of it. Now, if I or anybody else did something like that? I'd hear about it the rest of my life."

He snorted. "Anyway, thanks for the note. So you were safe enough. But you know what you put us through? Sure, we figured you were at the cathedral, but I want you to know that we went to the police station. The hospital. The hotels. Even the boatyards.

"But, seriously, maybe *you* should have been at least a little concerned. Even we were concerned. You know, there is such a thing as danger. Sure, you have your beer ministry, but still, buddy. It doesn't even compare. You know how dangerous it is around there? At night? Right before Christmas? You know they're talking about a riot down there on Christmas day? You should hear the stories I've been hearing at Rosey's. And that's where I'll be. No need to see this beautiful body being bruised, if you don't mind."

I was sitting back, relaxing. I was getting my weekly minimum requirement of Jack, Vitamin J, and it was working. St. Guayábe was exhilarating, but it felt good to be back home again.

Jack was going on. "Anyway, I don't know where you went off today either, but lemme tell you what you've been missing. Whilst you're off doing God knows what, you don't need to tell me --," holding up his hand to keep me from interrupting him, as if I or anyone could --- "you should have been out at Rosey's today. You really missed a show. This yacht pulls in. I mean, this was an ocean liner. The goal of our dreams of fabulous riches unfolding before our very eyes. You should have seen it. This *cruise ship*. And it comes gliding into Rosey's little cove. While we're all discussing how a boat that big can come in so close to the shore, the whole front of the thing lifts up, and a ramp comes out, like it's sticking out its tongue at us, and this barge comes rolling down the ramp, hits the waves, *crushes* the waves, and rolls right up onto the beach.

When it gets to the beach, out jump these three guys wearing the same color shirts."

Jack's eyes were glittering, and his hands were working.

"And then this fat guy in a bathrobe comes striding off the barge and onto the beach, like he owns the place, like he's the Emperor of Rome, and the three guys are attending to him, and then this beautiful babe comes along behind him, maybe three steps behind, and she's a stunner. And Rosey throws his arms out to greet this King of the Sea, and they hug, and they're going on loud in some language I can't understand, except it might be about drugs – drugs? 'droogs'? -- like that, like I say, it was some foreign language, and I can't read the name on the yacht or the barge either, like it's in Greek or something, or maybe Russkie.

"So Rosey goes trotting over to the bar, while the crew, the guys in the red uniforms, they've been setting up this tent pavilion, and then they haul a sofa off the barge over to the pavilion, and a rug, Persian rug, and a small table. So this fat guy drapes himself over the sofa, and Rosey's bringing a drink over to him on a tray, and his crew is fanning him, and the babe is sitting on the rug at the guy's feet. The only thing missing are the peeled grapes. Never saw anything like it in my life."

"How did that go over with the happy crowd at Rosey's?"

"Tell you the truth, we were just sitting there in awe. A row of guys with our tongues hanging out. Like a clothesline of red towels. One guy says, he's read about this act before somewhere, this fellow has to be some kind of Russian oligarch gazillionaire. He said you could rent a yacht like that for about half a mil for a week, which all of us together could do if we cashed out and then went on welfare for the rest of our lives. Al says, I think it comes with a car, and so Charlie says, what about the dame, is she part of the package?, and Al says, who knows, probably an extra-cost option, and then the old-timer, the guy from California who's sort of our natural leader, he says, for all his money we've still got the same beach and besides I'll bet ya it gets hot and buggy under that pavilion,

"And around that time is when the fat guy, the emperor, and I mean, he was round, like a pink beachball, he gets up and starts walking over toward the shore, and his crew is all just watching him, they're not sure what he's doing, and the woman doesn't know what to do either, so she just sort of sprawls out on the rug next to the sofa and tries to look alluring. And the fat guy just stands there, at the edge of the water, and the crew under the pavilion, they're just standing there, and finally the fat guy raises his hand and snaps his fingers. So the dame goes running over to him, and the crew starts breaking everything down again, falling all over themselves, and the next thing you know, they're gone, maybe spent half an hour at Rosey's. And we're all thinking, so that's what we're working toward. All that money. All that power."

"So tell me," I said, "how did you feel about that?"

"Kind of funny, actually. Took us about ten minutes before we could get back to discussing deals again."

"But you did get back."

"Yeah. Left kind of a funny taste, though. But then --"

Jack had been momentarily thoughtful. Now he pursed his lips, cocked his head sideways. He had another story.

" – but then we get this other boat. Maybe half an hour later. Harbor cruiser. Police boat. Big chrome siren, lots of antennas, a skiff bobbing along behind it. Three guys and a bossman again. Rule of threes, I guess, but no dame this time. When the skiff hits the shore, the one guy, the one with the weapon, and, when I say it's a weapon, believe me, it's a cannon; anyway, he secures the perimeter. The other two are in orange jumpsuits. Not your average tourists. Believe me, no one on the beach is moving. We're not breathing. So those two deploy into the brush behind Rosey's bar while the bossman goes over to Rosey's wife and they have a little conference. Did I tell you about her? Katenka, I think. She's a Russkie too, if I didn't mention that before, and she's the one who actually runs the joint. I wonder what she'd charge to haunt a house. Stay away from her, I say. Anyway in a few minutes these guys in the jumpsuits are back out of the woods dragging a big black garbage bag, and off they go. So up I go to Rosey: What's that all about? So he makes up one of his little songs right there:

Those men come for 'Mandy's stuff
Don't want no story, don't want no guff
They just tote it away, no more trace the girl
No sign of her here, or in the whole world.

"So I guess it's all about that Amanda broad and I guess her tent and her other stuff back there in the brush. Remember her, back at the airport? And then they're passing the hat for her, so she must be okay somewhere."

Before I could say anything, Jack just went right on. "Which, by the way, I have a little idea about those songs of Rosey's. What I'm thinking is .."

Jack seemed to be coming back down.

" .. what I'm thinking is, actually, me and Rosey, we're going to put together a little book of some of his songs, and sayings, to sell to his guests, you know, and with recipes, a history of this place, pictures, his football career – did you know he played pro ball? But we need someone to help put it together, and I figured you know a little about words, so I said that I think I know someone who could help. Whaddya think? When you come out tomorrow, I'll get Rosey and us together for a sitsee. Why not? You'll be there anyway. I tell you, it's a civic act to preserve these ditties, true charity, you know, so it's right up your alley. I've got a couple of pages of them in the other room already. Want to see them?"

"Not yet." Once again here before me was the true Jack, the Jack of old, the Jack I knew so well. He wasn't dreaming great riches or sweating the police now, just innocently pitching his next entertainment, which, to increase his joy, might be lucrative as well.

"I can even remember a few of them. Lemme think."

"And I'm going to get involved in this because ..?" I was trying to figure out how to phrase my question, which was, Would there be anything in this for me besides appreciation?

"Quiet, I'm thinking. How about this one? He's been singing this one for the last few days. Something like this:

All the mon that comes to here
They all chant from far and near
Sing the babe all the wise men there
They join the starry angel choir.

That sounds familiar, I thought. "You really think people will spend real money for that?"

"Come on, it's just a souvenir, no one's actually going to read it."

"And, what's all this about 'deals' anyway? I can't get over that you're sitting around in this paradise working on deals."

"Oh, yes. I mean, how much sand can you stand? So what we do is talk business. Take my buddy from California who's into electronics, and this gal and her father who are running a mill in North Carolina – they're making pullovers for that big outdoor business in Maine. There's Charlie. And Al and his wife, or maybe she's his girlfriend, because she's a looker and *just* a bit younger than he is, and he's a character, he's from Maine too, or Connecticut, something, wants to move down here and start a sailing charter and school. He's something, thinks numbers. Dreams numbers. Talks numbers. Man after my own heart."

"Let me try again. You come down here to sit under the swaying palms, enjoy the soothing breezes, partake of cool beverages, and talk *numbers*?"

Jack feigned being indignant. "Whaddya think there is to do all day? Lemme tell ya, the first week here in paradise was great. But, like I say, how much of this do you think anyone can stand? By the end of the second week, I couldn't wait for you to get down here, remember? And Mike? He wouldn't leave his precious car for even a day. But that's Mike, so what did I expect? Anyway, then I got you into the chachkes, remember that? and so ol' Jack gets an idea. I'm not the only guy down here who's getting bored out of his noggin, so I start talking around a little and, sure enough, before you know it, we got this little group going. Lemme tell ya, there's a lot of opportunity down here."

As I now learned, St. Guayábe was rich in opportunities -- native crafts, lumber deals out to the northwest (just have to get those Indians out of there, they're selfishly hogging it all to themselves), import-export, a duty-free shop at the main airport, because Rosey needs a manager there he can trust, try setting up one of those sheep ranches out there in Sherman's Gardens for tourists, maybe even a theme park, make it real environmental. And cruise ships -- anything connected with getting those really large cruise ships into here (just have to dredge out the channel through that coral reef that's in the way), a modern marina or maybe two, solar – lots of solar – out there in the boonies, desalinization, you get the idea? And would you believe this whole country has maybe two golf courses?

I agreed. "I see how you and your friends – associates – have discovered a veritable wonderland of glistening potentialities. But aren't you forgetting something? Aren't we leaving in three days? And don't these other guys have homes too?"

"I was coming to that," Jack said. "So let's get out of the clouds for a minute and talk real. We'll be doing this book when we get back home, of course. You can't really get anything done down here,"

Seeing the expression on my face, whatever it was, he turned serious:

"Listen. Sure, it's fun here, and you can get some stuff done, but forget it when it comes to actually spending any money in this place. With the politics around here? Spend every penny you've got just to get the licenses and permits, and that's after all the money you spent just to get them to see you and talk to you. Not a chance. You *talk* deals here. You don't *do* them here. You'd have to be nuts, like that crazy Amanda at the airport. You remember her, the one I told you about on the phone? With the tent? Sea life lady? Turtles? Tell ya, she wanted to set up a yoga studio here, had the plans and everything. Hanging plants. A tea bar. We never should have let her sit in with our little group. Believe me, the laughs weren't worth it. What's that look? Hey, we were really just trying to help .."

"For laughs?"

"Of course for laughs."

He turned serious.

"Jimbo, me laddie, you're still not getting this. Once you've got a few pennies in the bank, it's *all* for laughs."

"Anyway," he continued, back to normal. "She wasn't getting it either. So we tried explaining the deal to her. Don't do it, we said. Not here. You think she'd listen? Too much time reading those business books, I think. She just kept coming on stronger and stronger. All about 'Determination!' 'Perseverance!' 'Empowering yourself!' Couldn't stop waving her drawings and talking her business plan. Aw, give .. me .. a .. break. Even Rosey almost had to say a word to her. You think he had a business plan? He had a ukulele and a smart driven wife. So finally we had to move our little symposium onto Charlie's boat. Missed her, actually, but what are ya gonna do? Very serious lady. And the rest of it you saw. That nutball scene at the airport. But I'm serious about that book."

Should I say I'd just seen our Amanda? Or play it safe? I played it safe, at least for now.

"But Rosey's managed to be pretty successful down here. How does that fit into your theory. He seems to get by."

"Rosey? The mayor of these parts? Actually I *did* ask him how he does it. He says he doesn't. He's just a duck, he says, and he winks. He says, I'm all about floating, just floating. It's my wife does the paddling. He says she's really *churning* that water. Even he doesn't mess with her, he says. She takes care of it all, the money comes in and goes out, and he doesn't ask. So we're all set for Rosey's, right? Got your thing ready, your service? And then we'll talk, right?"

"Yeah, about this booklet –"

"First things first. Are you good for this service? It's important. Rosey's counting on you."

"I think so. Think I've got it together. Spent the afternoon on it."

"So you'll be there, right? No garage, no cathedral, no spending the whole day in prayer, or whatever you were doing?"

"Good Lord willing."

"Will you cut that out? Put the Lord aside for one day and just come out and do Christmas for us, for God's sake!"

And I said again that I would, a Christmas service under the palms, wearing shorts and a colorful short-sleeved shirt while a three hundred and twenty pound swarthy Santa plays carols on his ukulele and the rest of us get tipsy.

"So that's settled, right? Now, got one second more?" He picked a folder off the floor and pushed it over to me. While he talked, I reviewed the contents. It was receipts from the trip, notes, correspondence, worksheets. The gas for the trip. The rental for this place that Jack had arranged. The money they'd spent to get across the border. The plane tickets for the trip back home at the end of the week. Two tickets. Mike would definitely be staying.

Something was missing. "What about the cost of that midnight lawyer the other night? At the police station."

"Forget it. We'd be tapped out if we'd had to pay for that. But look who's finally dragging himself in here."

Mike had come in. He seemed to brighten up when he saw me. "Good day?"

"Yeah, had a few adventures. How about you?"

Jack burst in, you shoulda, this yacht, this *battleship* …

Mike waved him off. "Gimme a minute. Too hotsweatytired." Unlacing his heavy boots, he pulled them off. "Here's how stupid I am," Mike said, and pointed to his boots.

"What's that?"

"My boots. They're hot."

"But they're safe."

"Yeah? Enrique wears sandals."

"So? Wear sandals."

"Can't. Gotta wear boots. Safety. And it's a habit. I'm stupid."

He walked barefoot into the kitchen, pushing himself out of his mechanic's jumpsuit as he went. When he came back, he was in his underwear, with a pitcher of water that he drained almost with one gulp. He wiped his mouth with the back of his hand and said, "I guess you two can go outside now?"

"What?" said Jack.

"Outside. Sit in the van. You and Jim."

"What are you talking about?"

"Wait," I said. "I think I have it." To Mike, I said, "You're talking about this morning, right?"

Mike nodded.

To Jack I said, "Two nights ago, Mike and I were out in the van waiting for you. Last night you and Mike were in the van waiting for me. So tonight it must be our turn, you and me, to go wait in the van for him."

Jack groaned. Finally he said, "Ha. Ha, ha. But wait. Hold off, you clowns. Maybe there's an idea here. Just give me a minute." Finally he said, "Nope. Sorry, there isn't. No ideas."

While he was thinking, I was thinking too. I was thinking, my goodness but Mike can't tell a joke. And I was remembering back to the dream. There had been that moment of discordant drumming and shouts. "Did you guys come pound on the cathedral door last night? And the police didn't come over and hassle you?"

"Nah," said Jack, "We couldn't wake them up either."

"But Mike," I said, "How about you? You were safe tonight? What about tomorrow and Christmas day?"

"Yeah, Mike, take a word of advice from ol' Jack and take a day off. Just come out to Rosey's. You know Jim here is going to be doing the service out there tomorrow. You don't want to miss that. Jim, talk to this man. Tell him how even the Bible says you're supposed to take a day of rest once in a while."

"We'll see," said Mike. "Anyway, I got a lot to do." He shrugged and stood up.

"For crying out loud, you can't even take a break for Christmas eve? And it's not even safe where you are. Jim, help me out here."

"It *is* Christmas eve, Mike."

"I'll try." Mike started down the hallway to his bedroom, then stopped. "But don't worry about us. If Enrique's okay, then I am." And he disappeared down the hall.

This was my opportunity. "I guess later for me too," I stood up. "I'm all done. Let's see what a real bed is like down here. See you tomorrow," and started after him down the hall.

"Do you think he'll be there tomorrow?" Jack said, not letting go. "He won't be there. I'm telling you. And I tried. You saw me try. Works too hard. One more thing. Like I started to tell you, he's staying, with the van."

I stood for a second more in the hallway, and then came back into the living room and sat down. I guess I needed to talk about my plans too, whatever they were. This was as good a time as any. I could sleep tomorrow night. Sitting down, I said, "I'm thinking of spending more time here too. I'll be coming back with you. But I don't think I'm done here. Can I tell you about it?"

"Of course. Just lay it on ol' Uncle Jack. Listening is one of my greatest gifts. Why, as I was telling Charlie the other day –" Seeing the expression on my face, he stopped. "What's up with you now? Another nutball idea? Is my work with you ever going to be done?"

"I guess not."

"I knew it. I could sense it. The way you've been moping around. Like I told Mike last night when we were looking for you. I said, let's just bag it and go home. He's either dead or gone off on some crazy goodness thing. That's it, right? Either way, I told Mike, he's beyond us. When you get one of these ideas of yours. Just like twenty years ago. Nobody could say anything to you then. Why did I think you'd learned your lesson?"

"More like twenty five," I said. "But at least there's no baby this time."

The lady in white.

He gave me a long look and shook his head slowly. "That's my ol' Jimbo. So, what is it now? Make it quick. I may have more thinking to do. Spill, already."

The lady in white. Why don't I say something? But I can't. There's no time. Something else to talk about.

I took in a long breath and let it go. I told him all about the feast at Mike's garage and the dream, and what I thought the dream meant. I left nothing out.

Jack thought for a long time. Finally he said, "Sometimes I don't get you at all. What are you even asking me for? This sounds just like the last time. Remember how I warned you about her? And did you listen then?"

"So warn me again now. I'm listening."

"Sure. But first, answer me one question."

"What's that?

"ARE YOU OUT OF YOUR EVERLOVIN' MIND?!"

"Probably, but don't shout, you'll wake Mike up." I don't know if Jack heard that, because he'd never stopped talking, but he did lower his voice.

He said, you don't know this place, you don't know the politics, you don't know the people, you don't even know where to begin. All you have is a dream and a picture in your mind. Suppose these kumquats uptown know how to run their life without your help. Suppose you make a fool of yourself. Suppose they eat you alive.

He leaned in.

He said, suppose these kumquats down there in the park aren't actually interested in the cathedral at all. Suppose they really just want their protest. Have you talked to them? All you do know is what the police told you. Or suppose they do come in and wreck everything. Suppose the local clergy are totally against you. Suppose this -- suppose someone far more capable than you is already working on it, so, instead of helping, you just muck things up?

He lowered his voice a little more. He said, "Take the best case. Suppose it all works out just as you say? It's not going to stop there. This place is a powder keg. If you ask me, how do you know you're not unleashing some stuff that could blow this place sky high. You're throwing a match into the gasoline. And think about this. Do you know what else could happen? Some nutball sees what you're up to, sees where it could lead, and just cuts it off, just comes along and blows you away. You could get yourself killed. Killed! Are you listening to me?"

He said, you heard Mike. They've been doing this for so long that nobody really actually cares. I'll bet they just enjoy the fuss they're making.

"And another thing. What about your work back home? All that work you've got contracted? And how will you live? Who'll be paying for your groceries? Don't look to me, by the way. And what about everything else you do there? You think we don't need you? The guys and those dames at the bar don't need you? We don't need you on the Board of Supervisors for the next two years? Think about all that's going to come up. What happens to that? What happens to us?"

He shook his head. "So there's a few little problems. Now, tell me this: What's the upside? A meal? Noooo. You want a meal? I'll take you to a restaurant. On my account."

Jack sat back. "Lemme tell you," he said, more quietly, not noticing that Mike had come back out and taken a seat in the overstuffed armchair by the window. "When that attack squad came for that broad's stuff, it was scary. Even Rosey was ducking away and looking sideways. It's all love and flowers here, sure, but think of every cop you've seen since you got here. These guys mean business."

I thought of every cop I'd seen. The ones at the airport were approachable, and the fellows at the police station were courteous and helpful. But, all right, not the babyfaces in Canaltown.

Jack went right on. "Lemme tell you a story. Don't know if I ever told you this one before. One of my uncles used to be a merchant seaman. Oil tanker in the Gulf. I don't think you ever met him. One time they went ashore in Panama and there were bodies all over the streets. They'd walked in on some kind of revolution or something. So my uncle went to the captain and said, Let me put together a detail and go bury those poor bodies. And the captain said, No way, Charlie. If those people don't care enough to bury their own dead, we got no business being involved."

"Sorry we got you up," I said to Mike

Jack turned. "Oh, you're back. Help me out here. Listen to what this guy wants to do."

I had told Mike what I had told Jack. Mike nodded. "I think I get it."

"Well, I don't get it," said Jack.

"Be careful," Mike said. "Guy got stabbed a couple of blocks away after you left yesterday. Lots of fights around there all the time. These guys are serious." Mike got up and started toward the hall again. "Too big for tonight. Let's talk tomorrow. There's time. Gotta sleep now, okay," and he disappeared again down the hall.

Jack spoke up again. "So, what are you saying with all this? Are you still going back with me? Or are you staying?"

"Going back for now."

Jack gave me one of his looks. Finally he shook his head. "Listen, you think I don't know you. You're coming back here. And you'll get your butt shot off. You didn't hear a word I said. You married her too, right? You say we have about $4,500 left? So, listen, before you head off. Keep writing the Institute. Tell 'em how we're doing and tell 'em we need more. Tell 'em about the dragster. Can you get pictures of it? And, whatever you do, don't you even mention the cathedral. You got that?"

Good old Jack, I thought, but I was done for today. I agreed, excused myself and went off to bed.

Good and Faithful Servant

Sometimes events unfold slowly, sometimes they explode.

The sun was just coming up. It was the day before Christmas; Christmas eve had arrived. I was doing the dishes. When I say I was doing the dishes, what I was doing was excavating. Three week's accumulation of dishes, glasses, cups, pots and pans, and cutlery filled the sink, crowded the counter, and covered the table. It seemed like they had used every dish in the house until no clean ones were left, and then washed just what they needed at the moment. That worked for them. It did not work for me.

As I dunked, soaked, scraped, rinsed, stacked, and dunked, I could have been thinking about so many things: Rosey's and the service, the cathedral, the booklet, Mike's cars, the Institute reports, even Christmas.

But I wasn't.

I was thinking about Carolyn. The time that I'd promised myself had come.

I'd been thinking a lot about Carolyn since I'd arrived, mostly in the back of my mind, but I was realizing something that I had never fully realized before. She died happy.

She died happy. I still didn't understand how someone could die happy, but I'd finally realized that she did. She wasn't worried about herself at all. She was worried about me. That was what she was saying the last time we got to talk, but I didn't hear it then.

It was all so simple: Her life had become so heavy for her to carry that she just laid it down, let it float away, gave it up to the wind.

Would anything have been better for her if I hadn't insisted on marrying her? The more I considered what had happened, the more I thought: Probably not. Her path was so set that anything happening off to the side of it wouldn't have made much difference in the long run.

What about me? Was I wrong to marry her? Now that I'd written it all down, and particularly the part where we talked it through about marriage, where I proposed to her, I was seeing what that we did was probably the best of my choices. What else was I going to do? So how was our marriage a mistake?

We make choices, all of us. There's The Big Jack, her father, his choice, and how it had worked out for him. He'd promised Carolyn when he went East that he would come back to her in 5 to 10 years. That's the way it works, he'd told her. The corporation brings managers in from the rural areas because they're tough and willing to give their whole life to the corporation for nothing more than money, and then sends them back to pasture when they've lost their edge. That is, if they live that long. But he didn't. He chose death too, or it was chosen for him.

For some reason I remembered a fellow from back in the bar, the one who had all the ideas about the future of the sexes, and how he went off with that woman. And I did nothing about it, didn't try to stop him, didn't admonish him with moral imperatives. I just sat there and let him go. Make your mistake, if you have to, but learn from it and then, when you've learned from it, come back. I did say that, or something like that. I hoped I did.

Was that the best I could do? Maybe it was. True, I would have felt much better, felt I'd stood up against evil, fought the good fight. But anything I would have said wouldn't have stopped him, would have just made it harder for him to come back.

Is this something like what Jesus meant when He said, Don't resist evil? Maybe, but those words of His were still so deep and so elusive, too deep for me, and I was almost done with the dishes.

I knew I was thinking about losing my life to gain it. Handing this next part of my life to the Lord. Without reservation. Without hesitation. Someday, maybe, if I kept following Him, I'd understand His words in their fullness.

So, this cathedral idea. If my whole cathedral idea fell apart around me, would that mean that trying to make it happen would also be a mistake? Maybe, like I'd preached a few times, mistakes are part of the plan. Maybe Jonah was supposed to run away.

Good stuff there, but was I ready? Would I even do it? I'd already decided that I was going back to Taylor for now. I was going back because I had absolutely no idea what to do if I stayed. Going home, I told myself, I would clean up all those loose ends at home, make a plan, then return to St. Guayábe.

Would I even come back? Or just give in to inertia.

Maybe my big dream would end up nowhere.

Going back still didn't make much sense. Staying didn't make much sense yet either.

Maybe, I thought again, if I just live long enough and keep working at it, whatever it is finally all might make sense. And work was something I did know how to do. I said.

Anyway I was going to get back in the plane. I was going to flee, like Jonah.

The scurvy crew was behind me, the plank was before me, the sea was below me. Should I take a step? Would there be a big fish waiting for me below the waters?

Here -- a sudden intense feeling. And then gone.

By now I'd gotten the kitchen table mostly cleared. A spot of tea might be nice. 'A spot of tea.' I loved that phrase. I practiced saying it – Spot. Spawt. Spahht. Spt. Spit. Spoot. Toot .. toot.

I was still cycling through the fricative variations, not forgetting the percussive possibilities, when there was a quiet knock on the porch door.

It was the redoubtable Mr. Archer Hindman-Pryce himself, all of him.

-- I do hope I'm not interrupting. Yes, a spot of tea would be most welcome. And, the veranda would be quite a suitable location.

When we went out onto the porch, Mr. Archer Hindman-Pryce – "Oh, please do call me Archie" – eased into a chair, admired the view, complemented me on my appearance, informed me that he was acquainted with our tea-loving neighbor next door, asked after my friends, and then inquired regarding what I'd seen so far and what my plans were for the rest of my stay.

"Then do I remember," he said, "that you've been here for only a few days? But of course, that was you arriving at the airport, and all of that. Have you been able to see anything of our lovely country yet? In particular, are you aware of our world-famous Rosey's? I recommend it to all of our visitors. Aside from being an authentic Caribbean beach hut, it's a lovely place, and so much more sedate than its reputation might lead you to believe. And our Mr. Poitier is a lovely individual, whom I'm proud to regard as a personal friend. And you say you've seen our cathedral? A proud monument, one of our best."

"What's going on down there? Why is there such a problem?"

He sighed. "Ah, yes, our problem there. I'm not quite sure, but it's a problem for us as well, what with a steady stream of broken heads and slashings around this time of year. I gather it has something to do with a conflict within the community, but it's so hard sometimes to understand what these chaps are up to. So hard even to understand what they're saying."

"The police down there say they want to storm the cathedral and run their own service there."

"The police say that? Oh, goodness, perhaps I've been misinformed." He was puzzled momentarily, then recovered himself. "Whatever it is, isn't it fascinating if only in a negative sort of way? Whenever we get together, we humans, we soon find something upon which to disagree. And then we progress to hurting each other, with whatever tools are at hand to serve that purpose. And then, then, we build hospitals, and, may I say, churches, to bring comfort and recovery to the afflicted. I'm sure you see this in your work as I do. We're amazing creatures, wouldn't you say?"

I wanted to add that bars are even more efficient to the purpose, being places where you could be both beaten and comforted, but I was still forming the thought as he continued --

"And so it goes. *Sic gloria transit mundi.* We seem never to resolve differences. But I digress."

He looked at me squarely. "I must confess to you, Mr. Lawrence, that I have come today to ask of you a rather large favor, and time does grow short. Perhaps, before I begin, might we have a word of prayer?"

Something unexpected was developing. We bowed our heads. *"Dear Lord, in this beautiful place, a paradise to the senses, you still bring us to the realities of your troubled world. As you call us to harmony, we see tumult. As we, your servants, sit here on your hilltop, you call on us to be a light. Strengthen us in your service, oh, Lord. We ask this in the powerful name of your son Jesus, who tells us that prayers in his name will be heard and answered. Amen."*

"Amen," said Mr. Hindman-Pryce.

We enjoyed a moment of silence, and then another. Then, "What do you have in mind? How might I be of service to you?"

He put one arm under the other, resting his chin in his hand, the classic thinker's pose. "I fear, in asking you for a rather large favor, I may be understating myself. Please understand that in no regard are you under any obligation to accept."

"Please go on."

He rocked for a bit. Did I feel the porch rock with him? I took a slightly tighter grip on the arm of my chair.

"Before I say any more, may I count on your absolute discretion, as a gentleman and a man of the cloth? A deacon, I may recall?"

"As you say. Of course."

"My situation is, I might say, somewhat .. challenging. I fear that much may have to be left unsaid. I do hope you can accept what may not always be understandable. I believe that may be rather in the nature of your profession?"

"You have my assurance. Please go on."

Here we go again. *Just one more small step out onto this plank, sir, the sailors called out. If you don't mind.*

"As I say, it *is* a rather large favor. Perhaps quite large." Hearing no response, he went on. "Would you be willing to take a short leave from our wonderful tropical paradise to perform a .. how shall I say this .. a great and good service?"

"I'm being invited to leave?" I said incredulously. "Have I been a problem?" My mind raced. Was I being watched? Had I been seen trespassing at the cathedral? Had I said anything I shouldn't have to the police in the car at the plaza? What about Canaltown? Should I even have gone there?

"Oh, no, not at all. Certainly not. Why would you even think that? We will most certainly welcome you back, should you choose to return to our lovely locality. What we are asking for is an escort. Perhaps if I explain." He reached inside his tweed jacket and removed a large plain envelope. "Inside this envelope are two tickets to Atlanta, Georgia, and a voucher which will enable you to continue to a destination of your choosing. Which I certainly hope will bring the pleasure of your company back to us. I might add that these tickets are for today."

"Today?" Today?!

"I fear so. We have only the one direct flight every Wednesday, and any other alternatives for the next few days are extremely awkward in terms of time and distances required. Perhaps it's as it should be. 'If 'tis to be done, 'tis best to be done quickly,' as speaks the Bard."

"Two tickets?"

"To Atlanta, Georgia. Perhaps, if you know of someone from the Atlanta area, you may draw your own conclusions."

Amanda, I realized. This was about Amanda. But why me? And why so suddenly? And why was it seemingly so impossible to speak her name? I wanted to ask, to say something, to just yell, but I held my thoughts. My inner voice was saying, Discretion, Mr. James. Wait, listen, you might learn.

Just one more step out on the plank, please. Nice and springy, isn't it?

Mr. Hindman-Pryce was continuing. "All of our options have been considered carefully. On the whole it appears that a quick exit will serve everyone well and avoid some rather unhappy potentialities. However, we can certainly understand how this may not work for you. I must say that you are our best hope. I fear we must also ask you for an immediate decision. I do hope you understand. May we continue? I'm sure you have questions."

"Could you give me a moment? This is unexpected, to say the least." Come on, Mr. James, it's showtime again. He said time is short. We can do this. We've done it before. Badly, maybe, but we've done it. Think. Stall for time.

"This person we're talking about, the other ticket –"

"I can't discuss that."

"But you understand that there are some things I have to know if this is going to happen."

"Please do continue. I'll do my best to answer."

"Suppose when the plane lands in Atlanta, there's no one there .. to greet .. our party?"

"On that score, I am able to assure you that the necessary arrangements have been made. The family – I believe I can say 'family' – has been contacted, and they have assured me that they are prepared to fulfill their familial obligations. You will certainly be met."

"What about .. this person? Suppose when I get there, this person has a change of heart and refuses to leave the plane?"

"That possibility has been considered, and I am able to say that steps have been taken to ensure the safety of all involved. I should add that the ultimate destination in question is quite an affluent suburb and can offer excellent services, should they be requested."

"So this person will be removed, if necessary, regardless of any personal preferences?"

"Regretfully. When you leave Atlanta, you will be leaving alone. Under no circumstances will you be accompanied."

Musing aloud, I said, "Suppose, when I get to the airport here – not the local one, I assume --the other party is not there? My service is not required. I'm alone with my magazine and warm soda." What then, as if I couldn't guess. I was playing for time while I thought.

"I may assure you again that you will be met. At both ends of your trip."

"Suppose there's some sort of a scene. A disturbance. I guess that's a reasonable question."

He nodded thoughtfully. "Quite so, I'm afraid. The arrangements have been made, but when I return to my office, I will call immediately to reaffirm that the necessary people are in readiness. Is that acceptable to you?"

I still needed time. "You said time is short. How much time do we have?"

While my large friend checked his watch, I wondered what would happen if the people back in Taylor ever found out about this escort service. That might well be the end of my semi-formal religious career. Or, suppose, just suppose, our friend escaped from her fine Atlanta home and turned up in the Valley? I'm getting good at these 'supposes'. Suppose during the flight, while we're in the air, a meteor were to strike the earth and destroy all life on the planet, making a landing impossible. Unlikely, I thought; I should be so lucky.

"We do have a few more moments. More questions?"

"If I need to stay there in the Atlanta area for any reason?" By now I was just playing for time.

"There are funds in the envelope, and more funds are available if requested."

"Yes, what about the money? If I might ask, where is the money coming from?"

"The funds required have been contributed privately. I trust that no one should need to ask further."

I was thinking, Why the hurry? What's really going on here? I wanted to ask, but I knew I wouldn't get an answer, so I said, "You've worked hard on this, haven't you?"

"Myself, and several other concerned individuals, to whom a debt of gratitude is owed, I might add."

Another car had pulled up behind his about this time – a sedan, unmarked, like the one that brought Mr. Hindman-Pryce and his driver.

A thought had formed in my mind while I was buying time. What have I got to lose? I let it go.

"This is quite a favor you're asking. May I ask one in return?" It's time to think like Jack. Don't give away the store. Be a child of God, as innocent as a dove, but be as wise as a serpent.

Mr. Hindman-Pryce nodded, almost imperceptibly. "Please do go on."

"I've been thinking about the cathedral and the situation there." Mr. Hindman-Pryce nodded again, so I continued. "We were talking about the cathedral a moment ago. Whatever else is going on, why can't we all celebrate Christmas in the cathedral? Celebrate God's gift to us? Why can't those doors be open for a feast on this day of all days?"

"A hestiasis, you say. A gathering of the community. I must say, I rather like the thought."

"A what?"

"Oh, forgive me, I must be showing off my education. Of course, Hestia, the goddess of the hearth, in honor of whom the community gather for a feast. Please pardon me."

I went on. "And I've been doing more thinking. What can I do to make this feast happen? One thing I know is that there's no way under heaven that I can do this by myself. I'll need help."

He still said nothing. I added, "What is the terrible thing that would happen if we opened those doors for a day?"

"It's complicated, I'm sure. Rather like the situation I came here to discuss. You see," he went on, "we're rather at an impasse here in St. Guayábe, in some regards."

Take your time, Mr. James. What you say next is important. Think like Jack.

"Suppose we had some sort of a feast on the plaza in front of the cathedral?"

Mr. Hindman-Pryce laughed. "My dear fellow, you must understand that I have no influence at all over any of this." He was quite amused.

"I'm sure." I smiled too. "But I need help, any help I can get. And you need .. would appreciate my help."

"Well played. But I don't see what I can do for you, in exchange for my request of you." Puzzled, he was. "Perhaps, as your initiative evolves, I may be able to render some service."

"I have the same problem," I confessed, "I don't see yet what I can do either. No answer at all. At all!" I laughed. "I really have absolutely no idea what I'm doing. Maybe nothing." Maybe that's what He wants me to learn. "So, can I count on your help?"

He tightened his lips. He said, "Interesting. Quite. I can only say that my door will be open to you. I'm afraid it's all I have to offer now. May I await our further discussion?"

Then, "Goodness me," a quick glance at his wrist. "How time gets away from us! I really must be moving on. It is now 7:28. This flight," he held up the envelope, "is scheduled to depart at 8:45. If necessary, the plane will be held, and your expeditious boarding has been arranged. So, may I offer you this envelope?"

"Can I take a moment?"

I've had a few times in my life, and now this was another one. So, here I am, Lord. Is this what you want of me? Seems that way. So, say or do something if it isn't. Otherwise, I'm in. I guess.

How about my plans for this day? For a starter, it looks like I won't finish putting those dishes away. No Rosey? or can I make it back in time? Don't know; let go. If you want me for Rosey's as well. You'll let me know? No easy day, that's for sure. Find my pack, leave a note. Do I have any change for tips? Thank goodness the suitcase with the wine is all set up for Rosey's. Maybe it's better to bring it now; if I want to make it out to Rosey's at all, I won't want to take the time to come back here later today. No, wait, set out the suitcase and the pastries at the table and ask Jack to take them to Rosey's when you write him your note.

Just one more small step, called the captain. You'll find the water most cool and refreshing.

I looked my visitor in the eye. He didn't flinch. I hoped we had a deal. Like Jack says, if you can't get a loaf, try for half a loaf. But I knew what Jack would think about my performance just now -- some negotiator I turned out to be.

I hoped there would be a big fish down there, just waiting to swallow me.

And then I looked Him in the eye, as best I could. The Father. What do You think? Or is this Your idea of a trial run? Or is *this* the service You have for me? Only one way to find out. And, by the way, stop thinking 'He.' G-d is not a 'He'. Now, go.

I took the ticket.

A Few More Words From Jack

That's it? That's the end? That's an ending?

I don't get it. I told him that right out. And he says – get this! – that he doesn't get it either, he just did it, just took off with that crazy broad. And for what? At least, actually he did make it back to Rosey's. Almost gave me a heart attack, he was so late, but his service worked and the pastries were great.

Anyway, about his whole big idea about this cathedral down there and this big dinner for all the people, and he got some pastor friend of Mike's involved, and some guy from the governor general's office or maybe the hospital, and even Rosey, but then it all fell through, I don't know the details.

I wish I could tell you that this was the end of it, but it's not. No, sir. He's gotten worse. Now he thinks he wants to do something for those girls out at that place on the other side of StateLine.

I tell you, this religion thing is all good and fine in its place, but it can get really crazy when it gets ahold of you.

Are you nuts? That's what I said, right out. Have you gone totally *out of your mind? You know what they'll say? "Pastor found in whorehouse. Minister hanging out with prostitutes." They'll hang* you. *No one's going to care that you're only there to help. They're not even going to hear you about how a servant just does what he's called to do. I mean, they're just going to be all just too busy just stringing you up.*

Oh, and by the way, can I – me!, he means -- look into setting up some sort of nonprofit fund to help these poor kids out? He'll make sure no one ever knows about me being involved.

And I'm going to do it?

Yeah, I know it's crazy. But still ..

www.ingramcontent.com/pod-product-compliance
Lightning Source LLC
Chambersburg PA
CBHW061300210726
48293CB00003B/1043

* 9 7 8 1 9 5 5 5 8 1 8 9 9 *